CAMPAIGN • 247

SANTA CRUZ 1942

Carrier duel in the South Pacific

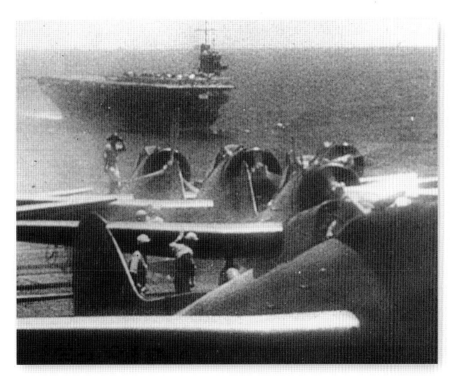

MARK STILLE   ILLUSTRATED BY HOWARD GERRARD

Series editor Marcus Cowper

First published in Great Britain in 2012 by Osprey Publishing,
Midland House, West Way, Botley, Oxford OX2 0PH, UK
44-02 23rd St, Suite 219, Long Island City, NY 11101, USA

E-mail: info@ospreypublishing.com

A CIP catalog record for this book is available from the British Library.

ISBN: 978 1 84908 605 9
E-book ISBN: 978 1 84908 606 6
E-pub ISBN: 978 1 78096 896 4

Editorial by Ilios Publishing Ltd, Oxford, UK (www.iliospublishing.com)
Page layout by The Black Spot
Index by Fionbar Lyons
Typeset in Myriad Pro and Sabon
Maps by Bounford.com
3D bird's-eye view by Ian Palmer
Battlescene illustrations by Howard Gerrard
Originated by PDQ Media, Bungay, UK
Printed in China through Worldprint Ltd

12 13 14 15 16   10 9 8 7 6 5 4 3 2 1

ACKNOWLEDGMENTS

The author is indebted to John Lundstrom who graciously reviewed the
text and provided numerous clarifications. The author would also like to
thank Robert Hanshew at the Navy History and Heritage Command
Photographic Section and the Yamato Museum for their generous
assistance in procuring the photographs used in the book.

ARTIST'S NOTE

Readers may care to note that the original paintings from which the color
plates in this book were prepared are available for private sale. The
Publishers retain all reproduction copyright whatsoever. All enquiries
should be addressed to:

Howard Gerrard, 11 Oaks Road, Tenterden, Kent, TN30 6RD, UK

The Publishers regret that they can enter into no correspondence upon
this matter.

THE WOODLAND TRUST

Osprey Publishing are supporting the Woodland Trust, the UK's leading
woodland conservation charity, by funding the dedication of trees.

Conversion table

1 inch	2.54cm
1 foot	0.3048m
1 yard	0.9144m
1 mile	1.609km
1 pound	0.4536kg
1 ounce	28.3495231g

CONTENTS

Strategic situation, September 1942

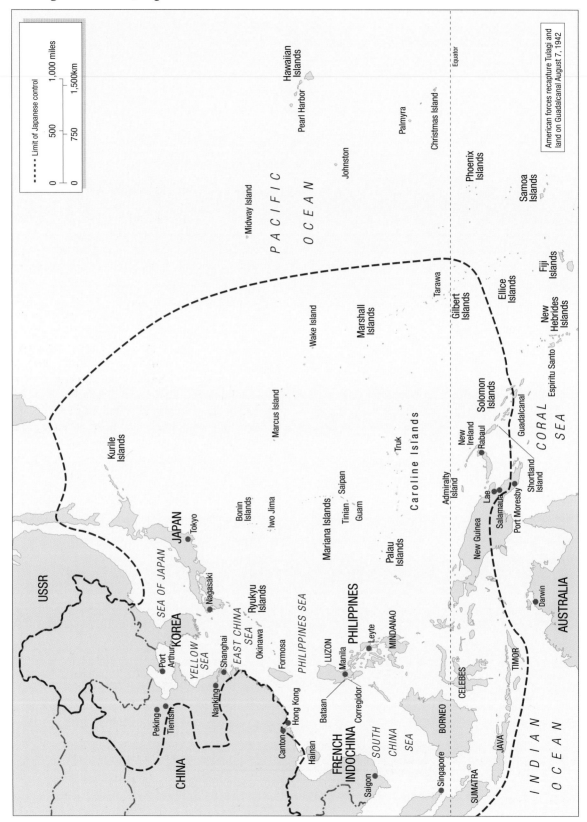

Limit of Japanese control

| 0 | 500 | 1,000 miles |
| 0 | 750 | 1,500km |

American forces recapture Tulagi and land on Guadalcanal August 7, 1942

Equator

PACIFIC OCEAN

Hawaiian Islands

Pearl Harbor

Midway Island

Johnston

Palmyra

Christmas Island

Phoenix Islands

Samoa Islands

Fiji Islands

Ellice Islands

New Hebrides Islands

Tarawa

Gilbert Islands

Wake Island

Marshall Islands

Marcus Island

Truk

Caroline Islands

Espiritu Santo

Solomon Islands

CORAL SEA

New Ireland

Rabaul

Guadalcanal

Shortland Island

Admiralty Island

New Guinea

Lae

Salamaua

Port Moresby

Kurile Islands

Bonin Islands

Iwo Jima

Mariana Islands

Tinian Saipan

Guam

Palau Islands

JAPAN

Tokyo

SEA OF JAPAN

USSR

KOREA

Port Arthur

YELLOW SEA

Shanghai

Nagasaki

EAST CHINA SEA

Ryukyu Islands

Okinawa

Formosa

PHILIPPINE SEA

PHILIPPINES

LUZON

Manila

Leyte

MINDANAO

DARWIN

Darwin

AUSTRALIA

TIMOR

CELEBES

Peking

Tientsin

Nanking

Hong Kong

Bataan

Corregidor

Canton

Hainan

FRENCH INDOCHINA

SOUTH CHINA SEA

CHINA

Saigon

BORNEO

Singapore

SUMATRA

JAVA

INDIAN OCEAN

INTRODUCTION

The United States Navy and the Imperial Japanese Navy (IJN) fought five carrier battles during the course of the Pacific War. Three of these are well known – the first clash ever between carriers in the Coral Sea in May 1942, the dramatic and supposedly decisive battle of Midway in the following month, and the largest ever carrier battle between a total of 24 carriers fought in June 1944 in the Philippine Sea. The two other carrier battles are not as well known since they were part of the larger Guadalcanal campaign and were not as dramatic or decisive. This was certainly the case for the battle of the Eastern Solomons in which five carriers (three Japanese and two American) fought to a draw in August 1942. However, two months later, in one of the most important battles of the Guadalcanal campaign, two American carriers took on four Japanese carriers in a battle to decide command of the seas around Guadalcanal. This was the battle of Santa Cruz, the third-largest carrier battle of the war. It was also a Japanese victory, but a victory gained at great cost and one that the Japanese were unable to follow up. Nevertheless, it is noteworthy that, four months after Midway when the Japanese carrier force was supposedly smashed, it was able to defeat its American adversary.

Enterprise at the battle of Midway where her aircraft sank two Japanese carriers and shared in the destruction of a third. She would also play a pivotal role in the Guadalcanal campaign. (Naval History and Heritage Command)

Neither the Americans nor Japanese foresaw that the Pacific War would be a war decided by air power. Neither foresaw that the principal naval unit would be the aircraft carrier. Carriers were seen as important, but still as supporting units to the battle lines. Both sides thought that the course of a future war would be decided by a clash of battle lines somewhere in the Central Pacific. This illusion was shattered on the opening day of the war. The commander of the Japanese Combined Fleet, Admiral Yamamoto Isoroku, decided that Japan's naval strategy of waiting for an American advance into the Central Pacific was too passive. He wanted to strike a blow at the opening of the war which would not only shatter American naval power in the Pacific, but also American morale. Having done this, Japan would be in a much better position to keep its wartime conquests through a negotiated peace.

Though he had difficulty getting his risky plan approved by his superiors, Yamamoto's vision of an initial powerful blow was realized in December 1941. The target of his opening attack was the principal American naval base in the Pacific at Pearl Harbor. The attack was successful beyond even Yamamoto's dreams and resulted in five American battleships destroyed or sunk in exchange for only minor Japanese losses. The agent of this destruction was the Japanese carrier force known as the Kido Butai (literally Mobile Force, but better rendered as Striking Force). The Japanese were the first to assemble multiple carriers into a single operational entity. The six carriers of the Kido Butai with its large numbers of modern aircraft and well-trained aircrew proved to be an irresistible force during the opening phase of the war. The Kido Butai ranged from Hawaii into the Indian Ocean laying waste to Allied defenses and supporting initial Japanese conquests which proceeded largely ahead of schedule and at remarkably low cost.

Japanese expansion in the Pacific was conducted under a joint plan agreed to by the IJN and Imperial Japanese Army (IJA). This plan called for two "operational phases." In the First Operational Phase, the Philippines, Malaya, the Dutch East Indies, Burma, and Rabaul would be occupied. As the Japanese moved to achieve their First Operational Phase objectives, Allied naval forces mounted ineffective resistance. The first large naval action of the war was fought in late February 1942 at the battle of the Java Sea. In this action, an Allied cruiser-destroyer force was defeated by a Japanese force of similar composition and size demonstrating the superiority of the IJN's light forces. Meanwhile, the Kido Butai provided cover for the invasion of Rabaul in January, the invasion of the Dutch East Indies in February, and then conducted a large raid into the Indian Ocean from March 26 to April 18.

After the successful seizure of the First Operational Phase objectives, the Japanese began to debate where to strike next. The Second Operational Phase was planned to expand Japan's strategic depth. Accordingly, eastern New Guinea, the Aleutians, Midway, the Fijis, Samoa, and "strategic points in the Australian area" were targeted. At this point, Yamamoto and the Navy General Staff began to have different priorities. The Navy General Staff, nominally the body responsible for the formulation of Japanese naval strategy, advocated for the seizure of key islands in the South Pacific to cut the sea lines of communications between the United States and Australia. Yamamoto preferred to give the priority to an advance into the Central Pacific. This, he believed, would have the added benefit of forcing the remaining units of the Pacific Fleet to give battle. In this decisive battle, Yamamoto was sure the superior numbers and experience of the Combined Fleet would ensure a Japanese victory.

During the first week of April, Yamamoto got his way, but only through compromise with the Navy General Staff. This compromise led to the Japanese attempting to conduct an advance into both the South and Central Pacific in the span of two months. In the first phase in May, an operation would be conducted in the South Pacific with the goal of seizing Port Moresby on New Guinea as the foundation for further expansion south. This would be supported by the Combined Fleet with the dispatch of one of the Kido Butai's three carrier divisions into the South Pacific. After this operation, key units would return to the Central Pacific for a powerful operation against the American-held atoll of Midway in the Central Pacific only 1,300 miles from Hawaii and against selected points in the Aleutian Islands chain.

The Commander of the US Pacific Fleet, Chester Nimitz, decided to contest both Japanese moves aggressively. Two American carriers were dispatched to the Coral Sea to counter the attack on Port Moresby. The Japanese assembled two invasion forces: one dedicated to Port Moresby and the other to the island of Tulagi in the Solomons. These invasion forces were protected by a covering force of four heavy cruisers and a light carrier, while the carriers *Shokaku* and *Zuikaku* from the Kido Butai provided cover against intervention by American carriers. The first target, Tulagi, was seized on May 3, but after this the tightly synchronized Japanese plan began to unravel. The two large Japanese carriers entered the Coral Sea from the east, but, in spite of the fact that this was totally unexpected by the Americans, the Japanese carriers failed to find the two American carriers present. When the opposing carrier forces did launch strikes on May 7, both sides miscarried. The Japanese strike found only an oiler and a destroyer, and sank both. The American effort fared better when it located and sank the light carrier *Shoho*.

On May 8, the main carrier forces finally clashed. In the first carrier battle of the war, both sides suffered heavily. The Japanese carrier strike found and hit both American carriers. One, *Yorktown*, suffered only moderate damage from a single bomb hit, but the other, *Lexington*, was hit by both aircraft bombs and torpedoes and sank later that day. In return, the American strike succeeded in putting three bombs into *Shokaku*, but she survived. *Zuikaku* was untouched, but losses to her air group were very heavy and the ship was not ready for operations the following month.

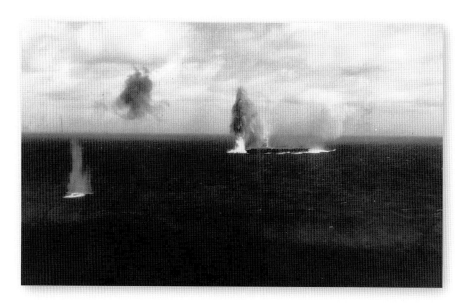

Shokaku under attack from *Yorktown* planes on May 8, 1942 during the battle of Coral Sea. *Shokaku* survived this pounding, but would again be heavily damaged at the battle of Santa Cruz. (Naval History and Heritage Command)

Coral Sea was not only a strategic defeat for the Japanese, but it undermined Yamamoto's upcoming Midway battle. All three of the Japanese carriers committed to the Coral Sea operation were unavailable for the Midway operation. This meant that the Kido Butai would go to Midway with only four of its six carriers.

American losses in the Coral Sea meant that Nimitz was left with only two fully operational carriers in the Pacific. These two carriers, *Enterprise* and *Hornet*, had barely missed the Coral Sea battle because they were conducting the Doolittle Raid against the Japanese home islands. The Pacific Fleet's other carrier, *Saratoga,* was torpedoed by a Japanese submarine in January 1942, and was still under repair. *Saratoga* would not return to service until late May. Even with just two carriers, Nimitz was still determined to contest the Japanese operation at Midway. Bolstering Nimitz's forces was *Yorktown* which was quickly repaired after she returned to Pearl Harbor following the Coral Sea battle.

Carrier *Hiryu* photographed from a Japanese aircraft on the morning of June 5 after being bombed by American Dauntless dive-bombers the preceding day. *Hiryu* was the last of four Japanese carriers lost during the battle. The catastrophic losses at Midway forced the Japanese to rebuild their carrier force. (Yamato Museum)

Midway was Yamamoto's personal battle. He planned the battle, went to sea to lead it personally, and committed the bulk of the Combined Fleet to its execution. All eight of Japan's operational carriers were committed, as well as 11 battleships, 14 heavy cruisers and the bulk of available light cruisers and destroyers. Once Midway had been taken and the Pacific Fleet destroyed, the Japanese would turn south to cut the sea lines of communications between the United States and Australia. Unfortunately for the Japanese, events at Midway did not turn out as expected. The plan devised by the Combined Fleet's staff and approved by Yamamoto contained fatal flaws. The only planning assumption that was correct was that the Americans would fight for Midway, but not under the conditions the Japanese expected. Nimitz had advance notice of the Japanese operation and intended to ambush the Japanese carriers. Between his three available carriers and the aircraft on Midway, he actually outnumbered the Kido Butai in aircraft. None of the other Japanese forces could support the Kido Butai which was also outnumbered in ships by the Americans.

The battle ended in complete defeat for the Kido Butai and the destruction of its four carriers. This was the result of inadequate staff planning, an inability to orchestrate defensive air cover, and a good amount of bad luck. The Japanese did succeed in sinking *Yorktown*, but their offensive power in the Pacific had been blunted.

After Midway, the initiative in the Pacific was up for grabs. Though the Combined Fleet still outnumbered the Pacific Fleet in every combatant category except submarines, Admiral Ernest King, Commander-in-Chief US Fleet, was determined to move more quickly than the Japanese. King had been focused on the South Pacific since the beginning of the war, and now, with the Japanese threat in the Central Pacific removed, he was free to turn his defensive strategy of guarding the sea line of communications between the United States and Australia into a limited offensive. As early as March 1942, King admitted that he had no intention of remaining strictly defensive but envisioned an offensive up through the Solomons to retake Rabaul.

Events would soon give King's intentions more urgency. On May 3, the Japanese seized Tulagi in the Solomons during their Coral Sea operation. On

Yorktown pictured after being abandoned on June 4 at the battle of Midway. The ship did not succumb until she took four torpedo hits and three bomb hits. *Hornet* took even more damage at Santa Cruz before sinking. (Naval History and Heritage Command)

9

On August 8, 1942, the first American offensive of World War II began when US Marines landed in the Solomons. Here, Marines land on Tulagi to expel the Japanese garrison. (Naval History and Heritage Command)

June 13, the Japanese decided to place an airfield on Guadalcanal, the large island directly across from Tulagi. On July 6, a 12-ship Japanese convoy arrived on Guadalcanal with two construction units to complete the airfield. By this time, King was already working with Nimitz to retake "Tulagi and adjacent positions." Once command arrangements were created to placate General Douglas MacArthur, in whose area of responsibility Tulagi actually was, planning proceeded with a target date of August 1. Guadalcanal was added as an objective on July 5 when American intelligence provided an assessment that Japanese construction troops were on the island. The required invasion force was rapidly assembled and planning accelerated. Delays in loading the assault force in Wellington, New Zealand, forced a delay in the landings until August 7. Finally, on July 22, the Marines departed Wellington en route to Guadalcanal.

The landings on August 7 gained complete surprise. The fight for Tulagi and neighboring Gavutu-Tanambogo was short and intense and both islands were soon secured. The Japanese construction troops on Guadalcanal offered little resistance, and, by the end of the second day, the Marines had seized the incomplete airfield. The Japanese air and naval response was immediate. Japanese air attacks arrived over Guadalcanal on August 7 and 8, but suffered heavy losses in exchange for a single American transport and destroyer sunk. The most effective response was mounted by the Japanese surface forces from the Rabaul area. By the evening of August 7, the Japanese had assembled a counterattack force, formulated a plan and departed to attack the Allied landing force. Despite being spotted by Allied reconnaissance aircraft, they fell upon the Allied covering force on the morning of August 9 with complete surprise. Using their intensively practiced night combat tactics, the Japanese sank four Allied heavy cruisers with no loss to themselves.

On August 20, the first Marine aircraft arrived at the just-completed airfield named Henderson Field after a Marine aviator lost at Midway. On the following day, the first Japanese attempt to retake the airfield with a ground attack failed. By this time, Yamamoto had assembled a large portion of the Combined Fleet, including the rebuilt Kido Butai, to support further reinforcement of the island and to destroy the American fleet providing support to the Marines. With three American carriers standing by to defeat such an attempt, the third carrier battle of the war was imminent.

CHRONOLOGY

August 7	Americans land on Guadalcanal.
August 20	Henderson Field operational.
August 24	Battle of the Eastern Solomons.

0935hrs – American PBY spots light carrier *Ryujo*.

1340hrs – Fletcher launches strike against *Ryujo*.

1400hrs – Japanese aircraft spot TF-61.

1455–1600hrs – Japanese launch 73 aircraft against TF-61.

1500hrs – Fletcher receives reports of *Enterprise* scout aircraft attacking Nagumo's carriers.

1550hrs – *Ryujo* attacked and later sinks.

1644hrs – *Enterprise* hit by first of three bombs.

1900hrs – Second Japanese attack wave misses *Enterprise*.

August 31	*Saratoga* torpedoed by Japanese submarine.
September 13	Japanese ground attack on Henderson Field repulsed.
September 15	*Wasp* sunk by Japanese submarine attack.
October 11	Combined Fleet departs Truk to support Guadalcanal offensive.
October 13–14	Two Japanese battleships bombard and temporarily neutralize Henderson Field.

October 14–15	Japanese reinforcement convoy arrives on Guadalcanal.
October 24–25	Japanese ground attack on Henderson Field fails.
October 26	Battle of Santa Cruz.

0250hrs – American PBY attacks Nagumo's carrier force.

0612hrs – Japanese aircraft spots TF-61.

0645hrs – *Enterprise* aircraft spots Japanese carriers.

0658hrs – Spotting report reaches Nagumo.

0710hrs – Japanese launch strike against TF-61.

0732hrs – *Hornet* launches strike.

0740hrs – *Enterprise* Dauntlesses bomb light carrier *Zuiho*.

0747hrs – *Enterprise* launches strike.

0818hrs – *Shokaku*'s second wave departs.

0835hrs – Ambush of *Enterprise* strike by *Zuiho* fighters.

0900hrs – *Zuikaku*'s second wave departs.

0910hrs – Japanese dive-bombing attack begins on *Hornet*; three hits scored.

0914hrs – Japanese dive-bomber crashes into *Hornet*.

0915hrs – First of two torpedoes hits *Hornet*.

0917hrs – Second Japanese aircraft crashes into *Hornet*.

0926hrs – *Hornet* Dauntlesses attack heavy cruiser *Chikuma* and score two bomb hits.

0927hrs – *Hornet* Dauntlesses score four to six bomb hits on *Shokaku*.

0930hrs – *Enterprise* Avengers attack heavy cruiser *Suzuya*.

0939hrs – *Enterprise* Dauntlesses attack *Chikuma*.

1004hrs – Destroyer *Porter* hit by torpedo from ditched Avenger; later scuttled.

1015hrs – Japanese second wave starts dive-bombing attack on *Enterprise*.

1017hrs – First of two bomb hits on *Enterprise*.

1046hrs – Japanese torpedo attack on *Enterprise*; no hits are scored.

1121hrs – *Junyo* dive-bomber attack against *Enterprise*; scores one near miss.

1129hrs – *Junyo* dive-bombers attack battleship *South Dakota*; score one hit.

1132hrs – *Junyo* dive-bombers attack light cruiser *San Juan*; score one hit.

1135hrs – Kinkaid informs Halsey of his decision to break off engagement.

1513hrs – *Junyo* torpedo plane attack on *Hornet*; scores one hit.

1541hrs – Two *Zuikaku* dive-bombers attack *Hornet*.

1555hrs – *Zuikaku* level bombers attack *Hornet*; score one hit.

1627hrs – *Hornet* abandoned.

1650hrs – *Junyo* dive-bombers attack *Hornet*; score one hit.

2100hrs – Japanese destroyers torpedo already burning *Hornet*; the carrier sinks early the next morning.

2300hrs – Kondo breaks off pursuit of the retreating Americans.

OPPOSING COMMANDERS

Admiral Ernest King, pictured here in 1942, was the guiding force behind US naval strategy worldwide. It was his vision to launch an immediate counterattack in the Solomons in the aftermath of the victory at Midway. (Naval History and Heritage Command)

THE UNITED STATES NAVY

The primary figure behind all US naval strategy during World War II and the driving force for the offensive into the Solomons in August 1942 was **Admiral Ernest J. King**. After both surface ship and submarine billets, he transferred to naval aviation in 1926. He earned his wings in 1927, and assumed command of the carrier *Lexington* in 1930. In 1933, he was promoted to flag rank and assigned to the Bureau of Aeronautics. In 1938, he was promoted to vice admiral and was appointed Commander, Aircraft, Battle Force. His career looked to be over in June 1939 when, instead of being promoted to Chief of Naval Operations, he was posted to the General Board. With America's entry into the war looking more and more certain, King's career was resurrected in January 1941 when he was appointed as the Commander of the Atlantic Fleet. No other admiral in the Navy possessed the undisputed toughness and leadership skills of King. Following Pearl Harbor, King gained more authority as the Commander-in-Chief US Fleet (COMINCH). In March, he was also appointed as Chief of Naval Operations, giving him ultimate authority over all US naval strategy and operations.

With his sweeping authority, King expanded the Navy's freedom of action in the Pacific, which, under the "Germany First" strategy, was clearly defined as a secondary theater. It was King that directed South Pacific strategy in 1941 and into 1942, not the Commander of the Pacific Fleet. He did not think that the Germany First strategy meant only defending key areas in the South Pacific and securing the sea lines of communications to Australia. Rather than conduct a passive defense, King was determined to begin offensive operations as soon as possible in the Pacific. The first step on the road to Rabaul was the invasion of Guadalcanal in August 1942.

The commander of the US Pacific Fleet, effective December 31, 1941, was **Admiral Chester Nimitz.** His early background was mainly in submarines, and later he served on cruisers and battleships. He had no background in naval aviation. Following the disaster at Pearl Harbor, Nimitz was the personal choice of President Roosevelt who had been impressed by Nimitz during his two tours in Washington. The qualities possessed by Nimitz would be in great demand as he tried to rebuild the fortunes of American naval power after Pearl Harbor. Besides being recognized as a capable administrator, his calm and determined demeanor made him the right person for the job. He also had an uncanny ability to pick good leaders and then

give them the authority to accomplish their mission. Another trait which became increasingly apparent was his aggressiveness and strategic insight. These were displayed at the victories of Coral Sea and Midway. On April 3, Nimitz was appointed as Commander-in-Chief of the Pacific Ocean Areas in addition to his duties as Commander of the Pacific Fleet. This made Nimitz responsible for the execution of King's plans to launch offensive operations as soon as possible in the South Pacific. However, Nimitz did not exercise direct control of operations in the South Pacific since this was the responsibility of the Commander, South Pacific Area.

Vice Admiral Robert Ghormley assumed the post as Commander, South Pacific Area on June 19. He held this position up until October 18, so he was in overall command during Eastern Solomons but was not present at the time of Santa Cruz. Ghormley was a controversial figure. While he has been described as possessing undoubted intelligence and a gift for diplomacy, he possessed no real command experience and was unable to provide confident leadership. The American campaign in the Solomons was a poorly resourced affair, and Ghormley was unable to work within that reality.

Vice Admiral William F. Halsey relieved Ghormley as Commander, South Pacific Area just before Santa Cruz. Halsey was the senior ranking US Navy carrier commander and, without a doubt, was the most aggressive. When Nimitz looked for an admiral to boost the morale of the men fighting in the Solomons, the natural choice was the flamboyant and ultra-aggressive Halsey.

The most combat-experienced American carrier commander going into the Guadalcanal campaign was **Vice Admiral Frank "Jack" Fletcher**. He was in command of the American carrier force at the battle of the Coral Sea and was commended by Nimitz for his performance. This success, and the fact that Halsey fell ill, prompted Nimitz to place him in overall charge of the American carrier force operating off Midway. It's important to remember the major role Fletcher played in executing the initial strikes which caught the Japanese carriers flat-footed. He was described by his peers as unpretentious and possessing strength of character, but tended toward caution unless he thought risks were warranted. By the time of the Guadalcanal campaign, especially after his early withdrawal of the carriers immediately following the landing, the criticism of his being overly timid grew louder. Fletcher had the backing of Nimitz, but not of King. After the Eastern Solomons, Fletcher was due for a rest period back in the US, and King made sure he never received another carrier command.

Rear Admiral Thomas C. Kinkaid exercised overall command of the American carrier force at the battle of Santa Cruz. He was a veteran of Coral Sea and Midway. When Rear Admiral Raymond Spruance was moved from commander of Task Force (TF) 16 following Midway to be Nimitz's chief of staff, and with Halsey still laid up since May 26 with a skin disease, command of TF-16 was given to Kinkaid. His peers described him as a clear-headed professional. Kinkaid was the last non-aviator to command an American carrier task force in battle. After Santa Cruz, he was relieved by an aviator. Kinkaid went on to have a fine war record as the commander of the amphibious forces tasked to recapture Attu and Kiska in the Aleutians and then as commander of the 7th Fleet.

The commander of TF-17 was **Rear Admiral George D. Murray**. He was a pioneer naval aviator and formerly the commanding officer of the carrier *Enterprise* and was close to Halsey, his old task force commander.

By law, commanding officers of US Navy carriers were required to be aviators. The captain of the carrier *Saratoga* was **Captain Dewitt W. Ramsey**. *Hornet* was commanded by **Captain Charles P. Mason**. *Enterprise*'s skipper was **Arthur C. Davis** at Eastern Solomons and then **Captain Osborne Hardison** at Santa Cruz.

THE IMPERIAL JAPANESE NAVY

The Commander of the Combined Fleet was **Admiral Yamamoto Isoroku**. He had assumed this position after being a Navy Vice Minister when he fought a prolonged action to delay the IJA's drive to assume total control of Japan's foreign and security policies. His assumption of the command of the Combined Fleet was an effort to get out of Tokyo and out of the line of fire of radicals who had threatened to assassinate him. Despite being a forceful advocate of avoiding war with the United States, he now found himself in the position of having to discharge his professional duties by preparing for the war he sought to avoid. He promptly proceeded to make the biggest mistake of his professional life by personally and powerfully advocating that the war against the Americans

should begin with a blow against the heart of American naval power in the Pacific at Pearl Harbor in order to crush American morale. Of course, the attack had just the opposite effect. Though marginally successful in a military sense, its political ramifications forever undermined any prospect of a negotiated peace with the United States. Nevertheless, Pearl Harbor and the ensuing period of Japanese expansion, cemented Yamamoto's reputation for brilliance while confirming his predilection for gambling. Yamamoto's performance after Pearl Harbor was less than stellar. His overconfidence led to the fatal compromise with the Naval General Staff which in turn led directly to the failed offensive into the Coral Sea in May 1942 and the disaster at Midway in June.

The defeat at Midway ended Japanese expansion and seemed to throw Yamamoto off balance. When the Americans grabbed the initiative in August by landing on Guadalcanal, Yamamoto was slow to respond. Though the Combined Fleet still possessed a significant margin of strength over the Pacific Fleet, Yamamoto always seemed one step behind during the Guadalcanal campaign which turned into a grinding battle of attrition which the Japanese could only lose. After presiding over the Japanese defeat at Guadalcanal, Yamamoto was killed in April 1943 when his aircraft was intercepted and shot down over the northern Solomons.

The officer in command of the Japanese carrier force during most of the Guadalcanal campaign including the battles of Eastern Solomons and Santa Cruz was **Vice Admiral Nagumo Chuichi**. Though he had no background in aviation, Nagumo was appointed in April 1941 to assume command of the Kido Butai. His command style was marked by overconcern with detail, a lack of decisiveness and extreme reliance on his staff. In spite of this, he led the Japanese carrier force to a series of victories from Pearl Harbor through the Indian Ocean Raid in April 1942. At Midway, Nagumo's luck ran out. Condemned by a faulty operational plan from Yamamato's Combined Fleet staff and sloppy tactical planning by his own staff, Nagumo's lack of aggressiveness was a notable factor in the Japanese defeat during which all four of his carriers were sunk. After the battle, he pleaded with Yamamoto to be given a chance to gain revenge, and Yamamoto relented. During the Guadalcanal carrier battles, Nagumo's caution was even more pronounced.

Nagumo's chief of staff was **Rear Admiral Kusaka Ryunosuke**. He had an extensive background in naval aviation, but he was not an aviator and did not possess a deep knowledge of aviation. He was cautious and outspoken by nature, and his cautiousness must have reinforced Nagumo's natural inclinations.

Rear Admiral Kakuta Kakuji was commander of Carrier Division 2. During the Midway battle, he led his force capably and covered the capture of two islands in the Aleutians, which turned out to be the only successful part of the entire operation. His performance at Santa Cruz showed him to be an aggressive officer.

Other important command figures included **Vice Admiral Kondo Nobutake,** who commanded the Advance Force after the Combined Fleet's reorganization after Midway, which actually included Nagumo's force. A member of the so-called "battleship clique," he was also known for his aggressiveness. Though he performed well at Eastern Solomons and Santa Cruz, in November at the Second Naval Battle of Guadalcanal, his botched tactics helped lose that pivotal battle.

Rear Admiral Abe Hiroaki was commander of the Third Fleet's Vanguard Force. He was familiar with carrier operations as he had been in charge of the heavy cruisers in the Kido Butai since the beginning of the war. Following Santa Cruz, he was in charge of the bombardment force at the First Naval Battle of Guadalcanal in November where his mission was defeated and he lost the first Japanese battleship of the war. As a consequence, he was forced to resign from the IJN in disgrace.

Rear Admiral Hara Chuichi, commander of Cruiser Division 8, was assigned to command the detached carrier strike group at the battle of Eastern Solomons. He had been commander of Carrier Division 5 at Pearl Harbor and the battle of the Coral Sea.

Carrier *Shokaku* was commanded by **Captain Arime Masafumi** who took command on May 25. He was noted for his extreme aggressiveness and did not hesitate to challenge Nagumo. He later died as a rear admiral leading strikes against American carriers in October 1944. *Zuikaku* was commanded by **Captain Nomoto Tameki** who assumed command on June 5. The captain of carrier *Junyo* was **Okada Tametsugu.** As was customary in the IJN, carrier captains were not aviators.

OPPOSING FLEETS

THE UNITED STATES NAVY

The carrier force

The United States Navy began the Pacific War with a total of seven carriers. After Pearl Harbor, the carrier task force became the primary fighting unit of the Pacific Fleet. Three of the seven carriers began the war assigned to the Pacific Fleet. Fortunately for the Americans, none was present at Pearl Harbor on December 7, 1941. The three Pacific Fleet carriers, *Lexington*, *Saratoga* and *Enterprise*, were soon joined by *Yorktown* in early 1942 and later by *Hornet*. The last prewar-built carrier to move into the Pacific was *Wasp*. After flying British fighters into the island of Malta in the Mediterranean in April and May 1942, she arrived in the Pacific in June 1942.

The two carriers of the Lexington class were the largest in the world at the start of the war. *Lexington* was sunk at Coral Sea. *Saratoga* was commissioned in 1927 after being converted from a battlecruiser, and displaced 48,500 tons. She had a top speed of 33.5 knots, but since she was the longest ship in the world, she was difficult to maneuver under attack. She had a disappointing war record going into the Guadalcanal campaign since she was torpedoed by a Japanese submarine in January 1942 and thus missed the battles of Coral Sea and Midway.

The three-ship Yorktown class proved to be a very successful design. These 20,000-ton ships were large enough to permit the incorporation of protection

Hornet joined the Pacific Fleet in April and had a short career before being sunk at Santa Cruz in October. The ship is shown here in May wearing her Measure 12 (modified) camouflage scheme which she wore her entire Pacific Fleet career. (Naval History and Heritage Command)

against torpedo attack. A 4in. side armor belt was fitted over the machinery spaces, magazines and gasoline storage tanks. Vertical protection was limited to 1.5in. of armor over the machinery spaces. At Midway, *Yorktown* took a beating from torpedoes and bombs in excess of the expectations of her designers before finally succumbing. The primary design focus of the class was to provide adequate facilities to operate a large air group efficiently. This design emphasis, combined with the practice of operating a deck park of aircraft, meant that American carriers routinely embarked more aircraft than their Japanese counterparts.

The Yorktown class also mounted a heavy defensive armament to counter air attack. This class represented some of the first US Navy ships equipped with the new 5in./38 dual-purpose guns that proved to be the best long-range antiaircraft weapons of the war. Four 1.1in. quadruple mounts were placed fore and aft of the island and 24 .50-cal. machine guns were originally fitted for close-in protection. By October 1942, the ineffective machine guns were being replaced by 20mm automatic cannons. *Hornet* received 32 20mm guns and *Enterprise* received 38. Both ships were also fitted with a fifth 1.1in. quadruple mount on their bows. *Enterprise* mounted the improved CXAM-1 radar. *Hornet* was initially fitted with the disappointing SC radar but then received a CXAM from the sunken battleship *California*. In service, the CXAM-1 was capable of detecting a formation of aircraft flying at 10,000ft at 70 miles.

During the Guadalcanal campaign, each American carrier embarked an air group of four squadrons. This composition was unchanged from the beginning of the war. One squadron was a fighter unit (designated VF and referred to as a "Fighting" squadron), two were equipped with dive-bombers and designated Scouting (VS) and Bombing (VB), and the last squadron was equipped with torpedo bombers (designated VT). By the time of the Guadalcanal campaign, the complement of a fighter squadron was authorized to increase from 27 to 36 fighters in response to experience at Midway where there were not enough fighters to fulfill combat air patrol (CAP) and strike escort requirements. Each of the dive-bomber squadrons had a nominal strength of 18 aircraft, and the torpedo squadron had 18 aircraft. The commander of the air group had his own aircraft, usually a torpedo bomber.

By August 1942, the prewar structure of the carrier air groups had fallen apart after the strain of eight months of war. Heavy losses at Midway and the wise policy of rotating veterans back to training commands had necessitated that the carrier air groups be rebuilt. *Saratoga*'s air group was composed of a collection of experienced squadrons. The fighter squadron was VF-5. Though the squadron had seen no combat action in the war, it possessed a number of experienced pilots. The dive-bombing squadrons included Bombing Squadron Three (VB-3) which had fought at Midway aboard *Yorktown* and destroyed Japanese carrier *Soryu*. Scouting Squadron Three (VS-3) had yet to see any combat action. The torpedo squadron was VT-8, rebuilt after it had been all but annihilated flying off *Hornet* at the battle of Midway.

Enterprise was the most storied carrier in the fleet. She had sunk carriers *Kaga*, *Akagi* and *Hiryu* at Midway. Her air group suffered heavy losses, and after the battle had to be rebuilt. For the first carrier battle in the Guadalcanal campaign, the fighter squadron was VF-6, which had experienced an almost total turnover of the veterans who fought at Midway. Bombing Six (VB-6) and Scouting Five (VS-5) from *Yorktown* comprised the dive-bomber squadrons. The torpedo squadron was VT-3, rebuilt after it was virtually destroyed at Midway flying off *Yorktown*.

When *Enterprise* returned to Pearl Harbor in September to repair battle damage from the Eastern Solomons, she received a new air group, Carrier Replacement Air Group Ten (CRAG-10). This unit was formed in March 1942 and was one of the first two replacement air groups. They were the first to have a number designation instead of their parent ship's name. The group consisted of Replacement Fighting Ten (VRF-10) under the redoubtable Lieutenant-Commander James Flatley, Replacement Bombing Ten (VRB-10), Replacement Scouting Ten (VRS-10) and Replacement Torpedo Ten (VRT-10). The air group was commanded by Commander Richard Gaines. Each of the squadrons possessed a cadre of seasoned aviators and strong leadership, but was filled out by a majority of new officers directly from the training command. When the new air group went aboard *Enterprise* in October, it dropped the "replacement" and became Carrier Air Group Ten (CAG-10).

Hornet's air group comprised VF-72, VB-8, VS-8 and VT-6. After a rough beginning at Midway, the air group was well trained, if lacking in combat experience.

The standard American carrier fighter from the start of the war through 1942 was the Grumman F4F Wildcat. The F4F-4 variant was a sturdy aircraft with a top speed of 278 knots (320 miles per hour). Its strengths were a heavy armament (six wing-mounted .50-cal. machine guns) and superior protection including self-sealing fuel tanks and armor for the pilot. However, when compared with its Japanese counterpart, it also possessed several key weaknesses. Its top speed was slightly less than the Zero's and its climbing rate and acceleration were dramatically less. The Zero was also far more maneuverable. The Wildcat's combat radius was limited to about 175 miles, making it the limiting factor in the attack range of an American carrier air group. Overall, the Wildcat was an inferior aircraft, but it could overcome its technical limitations with superior gunnery skills and better tactics.

The real stalwart of an American carrier air group in the early war period was the Douglas SBD-3 Dauntless dive-bomber. Given the troubles with American air-launched torpedoes, the Dauntless constituted the primary offensive punch of an American carrier air group. The Dauntless was a stable bombing platform, and, once into its steep bombing run, was very difficult to stop. It could carry two sizes of bomb. If a 1,000-pound bomb was carried, the maximum strike range of the Dauntless was 225–250 miles. A 500-pound bomb was carried on scouting missions, and in this role the Dauntless had a combat radius of up to 325 miles. The Dauntless had a top speed of 255mph

Saratoga pictured in 1942. The carrier was present at Eastern Solomons where her aircraft sank light carrier *Ryujo*, but damage from a submarine attack kept her out of Santa Cruz. (Naval History and Heritage Command)

and was rugged enough to withstand combat damage. Defensive armament included two .50-cal. machine guns firing forward and a twin .30-cal. machine gun fired to the rear by the radioman.

The new addition to the air group by August 1942 was the Grumman TBF-1 Avenger torpedo bomber which replaced the obsolescent Douglas TBD-1 Devastator. The new Avenger was such an improvement from the Devastator that American commanders were still learning to exploit its capabilities. Executing a torpedo attack at low altitudes and at low speed was a perilous undertaking, but the rugged Avenger improved the chances of survival, if not success. The standard American air-launched torpedo remained the Mark XIII aerial torpedo which was unreliable. Aside from carrying a single torpedo, the Avenger could alternatively carry two 1,000-pound or four 500-pound bombs. The aircraft carried three defensive weapons – a .50-cal. machine gun in a dorsal turret, a forward-firing .30-cal. machine gun, and a rear-firing .30-cal. machine gun mounted ventrally. The combat radius of the Avenger was slightly greater than that of the Dauntless.

The biggest question still facing American admirals in August 1942 was whether or not to concentrate their available carriers. Two schools of thought contended for primacy. The first, led by Fletcher, believed that carriers should be operated in the same formation to enhance mutual support and protection. This would allow for the massing of fighters and even escorts to increase the defensive power of the task force. This is what Fletcher had done at Coral Sea. At Midway, Fletcher's single carrier fought separately from Spruance's other two carriers; *Yorktown* was too far away for effective support and was lost.

The opposite view was held by most other commanders, including most of the aviators and the all-powerful King. They believed that carriers should be separated by 15–20 miles and operated in single-carrier formations. Doing so would decrease the likelihood that a single Japanese search aircraft could find both groups, and therefore increased the possibility that one group could evade attack. Aviators believed that operations by more than two carriers in the same formation were too unwieldy. At Eastern Solomons, *Enterprise* and *Saratoga* did not operate together, and *Saratoga* escaped being attacked. Aviators attributed this to the distance between them, but Fletcher believed (accurately) that it was because of the effective fighter defense.

Kinkaid agreed with the separation school. Halsey also shared this view. Halsey took the concept further and advocated a tactic in which carriers would be concentrated until they suspected or detected a Japanese strike to be imminent, at which time they would separate to a distance twice that of

LEFT
A Grumman F4F-4 Wildcat aboard *Enterprise* in April 1942 in early war markings. The Wildcat possessed a heavy armament and was heavily protected, but remained inferior overall to the Zero. (Naval History and Heritage Command)

RIGHT
SBD-3 Dauntless dive-bombers in early war markings on *Enterprise* during February 1942. Nicknamed "slow but deadly" by its crews, the Dauntless constituted the primary striking power of American carrier air groups during 1942. (Naval History and Heritage Command)

the prevailing visibility. This would reduce the possibility of the Japanese strike spotting both formations.

At Santa Cruz, neither concentration nor a more extreme separation tactic was employed. The two groups were operated only 10 miles apart. This was the worst of both alternatives. It was too far away to allow concentration of CAP or escorts, and not far enough away to confuse the Japanese. It was also far enough away to complicate further the coordination of operations, especially given the requirement to operate in radio silence or under conditions of bad communications which seemed to be the norm for 1942.

A continuing weakness of the US Navy's carrier force in 1942 was its difficulty in conducting coordinated air operations. Even at the victory at Midway, lack of coordination was especially prevalent. According to existing doctrine, once a suitable target was located, each carrier launched its entire air group, minus any fighters withheld for defense. This could be a lengthy process since it required the launch of two deckloads of strike aircraft. After launch, different aircraft speeds and altitudes of the various squadrons made it difficult to maintain a joint formation. Once bad weather and poor communications were thrown into the mix, the invariable result was confusion with squadrons ending up proceeding separately to the target. Doctrine did not even provide for the coordination of multiple air groups from different carriers even if they had the same target.

In the second part of 1942, the Americans were putting together the pieces for creating a formidable capability to defend their carriers against Japanese air attack. However, by the time of Santa Cruz these capabilities were not fully mature. The salient American tactical advantage during the early carrier battles was the possession of radar. All carriers and some escorts were equipped with radar which could provide warning of the approach of a large group of aircraft from some 70 miles away. This provided enough warning to marshal a fighter defense. However, early radar was unable to ascertain the exact height of incoming aircraft which precluded truly efficient fighter control.

Fighter direction was still a rudimentary art in August 1942. Problems with radio discipline hampered communications with fighters aloft and the few channels available often made control impossible. The performance of fighter defense at Coral Sea was poor, but at Midway progress was evident. At Santa Cruz, the fighter direction officer (FDO) on *Enterprise* was assigned as lead FDO for the entire task force. On October 23, just before the battle, *Enterprise*'s FDO, Commander Leonard Dow, who had been *Enterprise*'s FDO since before the war, transferred to Halsey's staff. Halsey said later that he debated this move, but Dow's replacement was the former head of the Fighter Direction School on Oahu, Lieutenant-Commander John Griffin. Despite Griffin's undoubted theoretical knowledge, he possessed no combat experience. *Enterprise*'s radar officer was also new, and, to make matters worse, other key radar personnel had also just transferred off the ship. During the battle, both *Enterprise* and *Hornet* experienced flaws with their radars.

Once Japanese aircraft broke through the fighter defenses, they still faced the antiaircraft guns aboard the carrier and its escorts. American antiaircraft defense doctrine placed the carriers inside a ring of escorts to increase the weight of antiaircraft protection. American carrier task groups maneuvered as a single entity under air attack to keep formation and maintain antiaircraft protection to the carrier. American ships were equipped with some of the best antiaircraft weapons of the Pacific War. The standard long-range air defense gun during the war was the 5in. dual-purpose gun. The 5in./38 gun was fitted aboard the Yorktown-class carriers and escorting destroyers. It was also reaching the fleet in increasing numbers aboard the new class of light antiaircraft cruisers and the new battleships. It was an accurate gun and possessed a high rate of fire. The escorting cruisers were equipped with the older 5in./25 gun, which was still a capable weapon but had a shorter range. Later in the Guadalcanal campaign, the 40mm quadruple mount began to enter service on the North Carolina- and South Dakota-class battleships; at Santa Cruz, *South Dakota* had four of the new mounts. This was the most effective intermediate-range antiaircraft weapon of the war. For short-range antiaircraft protection, two weapons were employed in 1942. The 1.1in. machine cannon was a four-barreled, water-cooled system that could deliver a rate of fire of 140 rounds per minute per barrel. However, in service it proved disappointing because of continual jamming problems. Last-ditch air defense protection was provided by an increasing number of 20mm Oerlikon automatic cannons. However, with an effective range of 2,000 yards or less, these weapons were unable to destroy Japanese aircraft before they dropped their weapons. Though American antiaircraft fire by itself could not prevent an attack by determined Japanese aviators, it did take an increasingly significant toll on attacking

LEFT
This is the port quarter 5in./38 gun battery aboard *Enterprise* pictured in February 1942. The *Enterprise* and her sister ships each carried eight of these formidable weapons which were considered to be the finest long-range antiaircraft weapons of their day. Above the guns are Dauntless dive-bombers. (Naval History and Heritage Command)

RIGHT
The standard long-range gun on heavy cruisers and the older carriers was the 5in./25; one is shown here on cruiser *Astoria* in 1942. (Naval History and Heritage Command)

Japanese aircraft. This culminated at Santa Cruz where antiaircraft fire took a toll on attacking aircraft equal to that of defending fighters.

Intelligence

For the first two carrier battles of the war, American commanders had been well served by their intelligence sections. While intelligence had provided advance notice of major Japanese moves, it was by no means omniscient. This was shown by the fact that at Coral Sea the path of the Japanese carrier force into the Coral Sea was unknown and even at Midway the full scope of the Japanese order of battle was unknown, though intelligence on the order of battle and intended operations of the Kido Butai was very accurate.

Going into the first carrier battle of the Guadalcanal campaign, Ghormley and Fletcher did not possess solid knowledge of Japanese intentions or their order of battle. Available intelligence was confusing; so unclear was Fletcher about Japanese intentions that he detached one of his three carriers for refueling just before Eastern Solomons. The problem was complicated when on August 18 the IJN changed its radio call signs temporarily making analysis of Japanese radio traffic impossible. As late as August 21, the Pacific Fleet intelligence officer assessed that the Kido Butai was in Japan.

The intelligence with which Nimitz and Halsey were provided before Santa Cruz was not only vague, but turned out to be incorrect. The Office of Naval Intelligence in Washington, DC provided a weekly assessment of the dispositions and intentions of Japanese naval units. In the weeks before Santa Cruz, these had been consistently inaccurate. Nimitz was able to warn Halsey of a major impending Japanese operation as early as October 17, but the estimates he provided of Japanese force dispositions were off the mark. Of the five Japanese carriers, Nimitz's intelligence officer placed only *Shokaku* and *Zuikaku* in the South Pacific. The two carriers of Carrier Division 2, *Hiyo* and *Junyo*, were still assessed to be in Japanese home waters. In reality, they had arrived in Truk on October 9. Light carrier *Zuiho* was unlocated. This faulty intelligence provided the basis for Halsey's risky plan of sending his two carriers into action well north of Guadalcanal.

THE IMPERIAL JAPANESE NAVY

The new Kido Butai

The Japanese carrier force had taken severe losses in both ships and aircraft before the Guadalcanal campaign began. For the first phase of the war from Pearl Harbor until May 1942, losses had been relatively light. This changed at Coral Sea in May 1942. During this first clash with American carriers, light carrier *Shoho* was sunk and all 18 of her aircraft lost, but worse was the damage to *Shokaku* and the loss of 69 aircraft from the air groups of *Shokaku* and *Zuikaku*. The bomb damage to *Shokaku* and heavy losses to *Zuikaku*'s air group kept both carriers from participating in the Midway operation in June.

Losses in the disastrous Midway operation totaled four carriers with all 248 of their embarked aircraft. As heavy as these losses were, at least aircrew losses were not correspondingly heavy. Still, 110 aircrew were lost and the survivors were exhausted after six months of non-stop operations.

The losses and lessons learnt from Midway required a wholesale reorganization of the IJN's carrier force. On July 14, the Combined Fleet was reorganized and the carriers placed in the paramount position for future operations. The First Air Fleet became the Third Fleet which was now clearly established as the Combined Fleet's primary offensive force. The Second Fleet, composed of fast battleships, heavy cruisers and destroyers, was to be used as an advanced screen for the carriers. This force was deployed between 100 and 150 miles ahead of the carriers. In this position, they would be in place to finish off any American ships crippled by air attack. Another benefit was that it would siphon off some of the American air attacks intended for the Japanese carriers.

Even after the heavy carrier losses at Midway, the Japanese still retained five carriers suitable for fleet work with another soon to be completed. These six ships actually outnumbered the four carriers remaining to the Pacific Fleet, but the aircraft capacity of the six Japanese carriers totaled about 300 aircraft, smaller than the total number of aircraft carried aboard the four American ships. The new Third Fleet was composed of two carrier divisions. The centerpiece of the rebuilt Kido Butai was the two carriers of the *Shokaku* class, *Shokaku* and her sister *Zuikaku*. Formerly Carrier Division 5, this was renamed Carrier Division 1 and was under Nagumo's direct control. *Shokaku*

TOP

Shokaku in August 1941. When launched, *Shokaku* and her sister ship were the most powerful carriers afloat possessing a fine combination of striking power, speed and protection. Since neither was present at Midway, both survived and became the backbone of the Kido Butai during the Guadalcanal campaign. (Yamato Museum)

BOTTOM

Zuikaku in 1941 showing the elegant lines of her design. Abaft the small island are two downward-sloping funnels which vented exhaust gasses. *Zuikaku* was the last prewar fleet carrier to be lost; she was sunk by carrier air attack at the battle of Leyte Gulf in October 1944. (Yamato Museum)

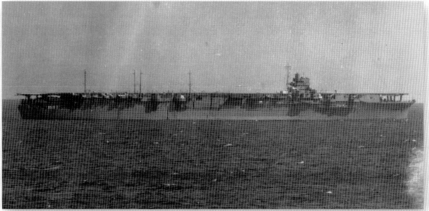

had been under repair at Kure since May 17 and would be ready by late July. Joining the two big carriers was the converted light carrier *Zuiho*. The old Carrier Division 4 was now redesignated as Carrier Division 2 and was placed under the command of Rear Admiral Kakuta. It included the converted carriers *Junyo* and *Hiyo* and the light carrier *Ryujo*. *Hiyo* was due to be completed in July.

Third Fleet also received an increased number of supporting ships, addressing one of the lessons learned at Midway. These included battleships *Hiei* and *Kirishima*, and four heavy cruisers (*Kumano*, *Suzuya*, *Tone* and *Chikuma*). The two ships of the Tone class were the most modern Japanese heavy cruisers and carried a large number of float planes (five) which were useful for scouting missions.

The only surviving fleet (heavy) carriers from before the war were *Shokaku* and *Zuikaku*. These were large (26,675 tons standard displacement) ships with an aircraft capacity of 72 aircraft. They were fast (34 knots) and well armed with antiaircraft weapons. Unlike other Japanese carriers, they proved able to sustain battle damage as proven when *Shokaku* took three 1,000-pound bombs at Coral Sea and survived. In August, *Shokaku* received a No. 21 radar with an effective range of about 60 miles against a group of aircraft. She was the first Japanese carrier to receive radar. The *Shokaku* class was the finest carrier afloat at the start of the Guadalcanal campaign.

The other two heavy Japanese carriers were the two units of the Hiyo class. These were not designed as carriers, but were conversions from the largest passenger liners in the Japanese merchant fleet. They were requisitioned in February 1941 and converted into carriers. *Junyo* was completed in time to see action at Midway, but *Hiyo* was just entering service when the Guadalcanal campaign began. Each carried up to 48 aircraft making them useful additions to the carrier force, but they were not as effective as design-built carriers. Their maximum speed was 26 knots, barely adequate for fleet work and their level of protection was minimal. Their machinery, destroyer-type boilers mated to merchant turbines, proved troublesome. This was demonstrated when engine problems forced *Hiyo* to miss Santa Cruz.

Light carrier *Ryujo* dated from 1933. The ship was designed with a capacity of 48 aircraft but carried fewer in service. *Ryujo* was an unsuccessful design with a relatively slow speed and unsatisfactory aircraft handling arrangements which impeded flight operations. On the other hand, light carrier *Zuiho* was more successful in service though she was a conversion from a submarine tender.

Each of the Shokaku-class carriers embarked an air group with three squadrons. These air groups were named after their parent ships and were permanently assigned to the ship. The composition of the air groups changed in light of the Midway experience. The fighter squadron was increased to 27 aircraft as was the number of dive-bombers. In order to increase the overall number of aircraft that could be carried, the number of torpedo bombers was reduced to 18. The reduction of the number of torpedo aircraft also reflected the Japanese belief that these aircraft were more vulnerable. The aircraft complement of the two Hiyo-class carriers reflected the same priorities as the Shokaku-class ships. Each of these converted carriers carried 48 aircraft broken down into 21 fighters, 18 dive-bombers, and nine torpedo planes. The aircraft of the two light carriers reflected their new air defense mission. *Ryujo* carried 24 fighters and nine torpedo planes while *Zuiho* carried 21 and six, respectively.

The post-Midway reorganization was still under way when the Americans landed on Guadalcanal. For the first Japanese offensive against the Americans in the South Pacific, Yamamoto could bring only Carrier Division 1 into action with *Shokaku*, *Zuikaku* and *Ryujo*. To put 177 aircraft on these ships, the Japanese had to strip *Hiyo*, *Junyo* and *Zuiho* of fighters and dive-bombers making them 29 fighters and 16 dive-bombers short of establishment (though they did retain an extra 15 torpedo planes). Carrier Division 2 would take

TOP
This is a photo of *Junyo* taken on June 3, 1944. Her appearance was similar in October 1942, but she lacked the radar mounted on the island. This view clearly shows her lineage as a merchant ship, but also demonstrates her large size which enabled her to carry a relatively large air group. (Yamato Museum)

BOTTOM
Ryujo after her second major refit in 1936 to correct stability problems. As designed, *Ryujo* was to carry 48 aircraft, but she carried far fewer in service. The ship was assigned to secondary duties in the first part of the war because of her small aircraft capacity and inefficient layout which hampered flight operations. At the battle of the Eastern Solomons, she carried only 24 Zero fighters and nine Type 97 attack planes. (Yamato Museum)

until September to achieve readiness, and thus was totally available by the time of Santa Cruz in October.

Carrier Division 2 arrived at Truk on October 9 after completing training in the Inland Sea. Both ships had a full-strength air group with the exception of *Junyo* which was deficient by three fighters. Both of the fighter squadrons contained a large number of veterans, and the attack squadrons were also led by experienced aviators.

Japanese carrier air groups remained superior to their American counterparts throughout 1942 in two areas – fighters and torpedo bombers. The Japanese dive-bomber was also a capable design, but was inferior overall to the American Dauntless. The Japanese used a design philosophy that stressed maneuverability and range. This gave Japanese carrier aircraft superior range compared with their American counterparts, but this was achieved at the cost of inferior protection.

The standard Japanese carrier fighter was the A6M Type 0 (called "Zero" by both sides). The Zero had met the Wildcat for the first time at Coral Sea and its superiority was acknowledged even by the Americans. It possessed exceptional maneuverability, great climb and acceleration, and a powerful armament. However, this performance was largely achieved by lightening

the airframe as much as possible which translated into a lack of armored protection and self-sealing fuel tanks.

The Japanese called their dive-bombers "carrier bombers." The standard carrier bomber through 1942 was D3A1 Type 99 Carrier Bomber (later codenamed "Val" by the Allies). The Type 99 was well designed for conducting precision dive-bombing attacks. It was a deadly weapon in the hands of an experienced pilot as proven by the fact that it had sunk more Allied ships than any other Japanese aircraft up to this period of the war. Though rugged enough to withstand up to 80-degree dives, it did not carry self-sealing fuel tanks and carried a smaller bomb load than the Dauntless.

The real edge possessed by Japanese air groups during the Guadalcanal campaign was the fact that they possessed a viable torpedo attack capability. This was provided by the B5N2 Type 97 Carrier Attack Plane. Later codenamed "Kate" by the Allies, this aircraft was primarily designed to act as a torpedo bomber, but could also carry bombs. The Type 97 was inferior in performance to the new American Avenger, but what made the Japanese torpedo bomber so formidable was that it could employ a dependable air-launched torpedo. This was the Type 91 Mod 3 Air Torpedo which contained a 529-pound warhead and was capable of traveling at 42 knots for up to 2,000 yards. The importance of the combination of the Type 97 and its reliable and effective torpedo cannot be understated. Both at Coral Sea and Midway, this combination gave Japanese air groups an effective ship-killing power not possessed by American carriers of the day. At both battles, once an American carrier was struck by an air-launched torpedo, it did not escape destruction. However, the Type 97 (like any torpedo bomber) was required to fly relatively low and slow toward the target making it very vulnerable to enemy fire. This weakness was exacerbated by the fact that the aircraft had exchanged range for a lack of protection.

The Japanese carrier force changed its doctrine and tactics after Midway. In each of the two carrier divisions, the two heavy carriers were seen as offensive platforms while the light carrier was to be used primarily as a

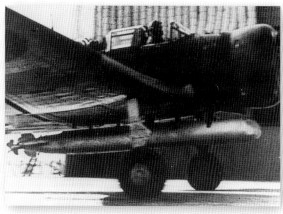

provider of fighters for CAP. Despite heavy losses, an important strength of the Kido Butai was its ability to conduct coordinated, large-scale, air operations. Going into the Guadalcanal campaign, the Japanese had shown they were able routinely to orchestrate air attacks by multiple carriers. Unlike their American counterparts, Japanese carriers did not operate as single tactical units. Rather, all carriers in a carrier division acted as a single unit and routinely operated their aircraft as a single tactical unit. This meant that, during the course of 1942, the Japanese were able to handle their carrier aircraft in a manner far superior to that of the Americans. Japanese offensive air operations were better coordinated, and because they did not depend on a single carrier, were usually larger.

Another lesson from Midway was the vulnerability of torpedo bombers. During the first part of the war, Japanese tactics when attacking heavily defended naval targets were to attack simultaneously with dive and torpedo bombers to overwhelm the defenses and minimize losses to the more vulnerable torpedo bombers. Going into the Guadalcanal campaign, the Japanese decided to hold their torpedo aircraft in reserve until the dive-bombers had crippled the American carriers. This tactic proved unsuccessful at Eastern Solomons, and by the time of Santa Cruz the Japanese had returned to their more traditional combined-arms attack with simultaneous dive and torpedo bomber attacks.

These tactics had a probability of success as long as they were being executed by highly trained and aggressive aircrew. By August 1942, Japanese carrier air groups still possessed these types of aircrew in abundance. Overall, they possessed a higher level of training and experience than American air groups of the period.

Throughout the first phase of the war, at Coral Sea, and to a lesser degree at Midway, the Kido Butai had shown itself to be a formidable offensive weapon. This was in accordance with the IJN's overall emphasis on the offensive. However, though the Japanese were demonstrably proficient at massing and coordinating offensive air power, they also demonstrated an inability to defend their carriers properly. This weakness was laid bare at Midway when lack of radar, poor CAP doctrine, weak antiaircraft capabilities and weaknesses in damage control combined to destroy four carriers.

At Midway, the most glaring weakness was a lack of early warning. Each of the four Japanese carriers sunk during the battle had been surprised by American dive-bombers taking them under attack. The principal reason was the total lack of radar on any Kido Butai ship during the battle. *Shokaku* was equipped with radar before Eastern Solomons. However, since the equipment was still new in fleet use, it did not provide complete coverage. It was used with some success at Santa Cruz and the employment of the Advance Force tactics which acted as an air defense picket greatly diminished the likelihood that Japanese carriers would be totally surprised as at Midway.

Direction for Japanese fighters performing CAP was still a problem. The Japanese used a system of standing CAP with additional fighters on alert to scramble as needed. True fighter control was impossible because Japanese aircraft radios were virtually worthless making it impossible to control aircraft once airborne.

All Japanese carriers were equipped with long-range (5in. guns) antiaircraft weapons and short-range 25mm guns. The 5in. gun was the Type 89 dual mount, but the effectiveness of this weapon was handicapped by inadequate fire-control systems and a doctrine which called for barrage fire against quickly maneuvering targets. The Type 96 25mm gun served as the short-range weapon and was fitted on all carriers and escorts in both double and triple mounts. Unfortunately for the Japanese, the selection of this weapon proved to be a poor choice since it possessed a number of weaknesses. These included an inability to handle high-speed targets (it could not be trained or elevated fast enough and its sights were inadequate), excessive vibration and muzzle blast which affected accuracy, and an inability to maintain high rates of fire because of the need constantly to change magazines. Because the gun fired such a small shell (.6 pounds), it lacked stopping power against the rugged American Dauntless and Avenger. As a result, American aircraft losses to antiaircraft fire were low.

The weakness of Japanese shipboard antiaircraft gunnery meant that the most effective form of defense from American air attack was skillful maneuvering. When Japanese carriers came under air attack, the ability of the carrier's captain to execute timely maneuvers was critical. The escorts around the carrier were expected to allow it to execute whatever maneuvers were required. Radical maneuvering made it more difficult for the carrier's gun crews to generate correct fire-control solutions for accurate antiaircraft fire. The primary threat from American carriers was posed by the accurate Dauntless dive-bomber; on the other hand, the American Mark 13 air-launched torpedo could easily be defeated by timely maneuvers since its top speed was only 33 knots. The faster Japanese carriers had the speed simply to outrun the torpedo.

Intelligence

The Japanese had only a vague notion about the intentions and operations of American carriers. They had no ability to read American codes, but analysis of radio traffic did provide indications of impending operations. For example, when *Enterprise* departed Pearl Harbor in mid-October following repairs after Eastern Solomons, the Japanese correctly deduced she was headed for the South Pacific. The best sources of information on major American fleet movements were spotting reports from long-range flying boats from the Shortlands. In addition, float planes from battleships and cruisers performed tactical scouting and performed well in this role. Japanese analysis of the basic American carrier order of battle was weak. By Santa Cruz, the Japanese believed that the Americans had already produced a second and third generation of carriers with the same names of carriers previously sunk which prevented them from even understanding how many carriers the Americans had available for operations.

ORDERS OF BATTLE
THE BATTLE OF THE EASTERN SOLOMONS
All strengths as of 0500hrs, August 24, 1942

( ) denotes operational aircraft

IMPERIAL JAPANESE NAVY

Third Fleet (Main Body) (Vice Admiral Nagumo Chuichi aboard carrier *Shokaku*)

Carrier Division 1 (Nagumo)

Carrier *Shokaku* (Captain Arima Masafumi)

       Shokaku Air Group Commander (Lieutenant-Commander Seki Mamoru)

       Shokaku Carrier Fighter Unit 27 (26) Type 0

       Shokaku Carrier Bomber Unit 27 (27) Type 99

       Shokaku Carrier Attack Unit 18 (18) Type 97

Carrier *Zuikaku* (Captain Notomo Tameteru)

       Zuikaku Air Group Commander (Lieutenant-Commander Takahashi Sadamu)

       Zuikaku Carrier Fighter Unit 27 (25) Type 0

       Zuikaku Carrier Bomber Unit 27 (27) Type 99

       Zuikaku Carrier Attack Unit 18 (18) Type 97

Destroyers (from Destroyer Divisions 10 and 16): *Kazegumo, Yugumo, Makigumo, Akigumo, Hatsukaze, Akizuki*

Vanguard Force (Rear Admiral Abe Hiroaki in *Hiei*)

Battleship Division 11

       Battleships: *Hiei, Kirishima*

Cruiser Division 7

       Heavy cruisers: *Kumano, Suzuya*

Cruiser Division 8

       Heavy cruiser *Chikuma*

Destroyer Squadron 10

       Light cruiser *Nagara*

       Destroyers from Destroyer Divisions 4 and 17: *Nowaki, Maikaze, Tanikaze*

Detached Carrier Strike Force (Rear Admiral Hara Chuichi in *Tone*)

Light carrier *Ryujo* (Captain Kato Tadao)

       Ryujo Air Group Commander (Lieutenant Notomi Kenjiro)

       Ryujo Carrier Fighter Unit 24 (23) Type 0

       Ryujo Carrier Attack Unit 9 (9) Type 97

Heavy cruiser *Tone*

Destroyers (from Destroyer Division 16): *Amatsukaze, Tokitsukaze*

Advance Force (Vice Admiral Kondo Nobutake in *Atago*)

Cruiser Division 4

       Heavy cruisers: *Atago, Maya, Takao*

Cruiser Division 5

       Heavy cruisers: *Haguro, Myoko*

Destroyer Squadron 4

       Light cruiser *Yura*

       Destroyers from Destroyer Divisions 9 and 15: *Kuroshio, Oyashio, Hayashio, Minegumo, Natsugumo, Asagumo*

Seaplane carrier *Chitose* with 22 aircraft

UNITED STATES NAVY

Task Force 61 (Vice Admiral Frank Jack Fletcher)

Task Force 11 (Fletcher)

Saratoga (Captain Dewitt C. Ramsey)

       Saratoga Air Group (Commander Harry D. Felt) 1 (1) SBD-3

Fighting Five 27 (27) F4F-4
Bombing Three 17 (17) SBD-3
Scouting Three 15 (15) SBD-3
Torpedo Eight 13 (13) TBF-1
Utility Unit 1 (1) F4F-7
Heavy cruisers: *Minneapolis, New Orleans*, HMAS *Australia*
Light cruiser: HMAS *Hobart*
Destroyer Squadron 1
Destroyers: *Phelps, Farragut, Worden, Macdonough, Dewey, Patterson, Bagley*

Task Force 16 (Rear Admiral Thomas C. Kinkaid)
Enterprise (Captain Arthur C. Davis)
  Enterprise Air Group (Lieutenant-Commander Maxwell F. Leslie)
  Fighting Six 29 (28) F4F-4
  Bombing Six 17 (17) SBD-3
  Scouting Five 18 (16) SBD-3
  Torpedo Three 15 (15) TBF-1
  Utility Unit 1 (1) F4F-7
Battleship: *North Carolina*
Heavy cruiser: *Portland*
Light cruiser: *Atlanta*
Destroyer Squadron 6
  Destroyers: *Balch, Benham, Maury, Ellet, Grayson, Monssen*

THE BATTLE OF SANTA CRUZ
All strengths as of 0500hrs, October 26, 1942
( ) denotes operational aircraft

IMPERIAL JAPANESE NAVY

Support Force (Vice Admiral Kondo Nobutake in *Atago*)
Advance Force (Kondo)
Carrier Division 2 (Rear Admiral Kakuta Kakuji in *Junyo*)
Carrier *Junyo* (Captain Okada Tametsugu)
  Junyo Air Group Commander (Lieutenant Shiga Yoshio)
  Junyo Carrier Fighter Unit 20 (20) Type 0
  Junyo Carrier Bomber Unit 18 (17) Type 99
  Junyo Carrier Attack Unit 7 (7) Type 97
Carrier *Hiyo* and destroyers *Isonami* and *Inazuma* detached October 22 for Truk
Battleship Division 3
  Battleships: *Kongo, Haruna*
Cruiser Division 4
  Heavy cruisers: *Atago, Takao*
Cruiser Division 5
  Heavy cruisers: *Maya, Myoko*
Destroyer Squadron 4
  Light cruiser *Isuzu*
  Destroyers from Destroyer Divisions 15, 24 and 31: *Kuroshio, Oyashio, Hayashio,*
Kawakaze, Suzukaze, Umikaze, Naganami, Takanami, Makinami

Third Fleet (Main Body) (Vice Admiral Nagumo Chuichi aboard carrier *Shokaku*)
Carrier Division 1 (Nagumo)
Carrier *Shokaku* (Captain Arima Masafumi)
  Shokaku Air Group Commander (Lieutenant-Commander Seki Mamoru)
  Shokaku Carrier Fighter Unit 22 (18) Type 0
  Shokaku Carrier Bomber Unit 21 (21) Type 99
  Shokaku Carrier Attack Unit 24 (24) Type 97

Carrier *Zuikaku* (Captain Notomo Tameteru)
  Zuikaku Air Group Commander (Lieutenant-Commander Takahashi Sadamu)
  Zuikaku Carrier Fighter Unit 21 (20) Type 0
  Zuikaku Carrier Bomber Unit 24 (22) Type 99
  Zuikaku Carrier Attack Unit 20 (20) Type 97
Light Carrier *Zuiho* (Captain Obayashi Sueo)
  Zuiho Air Group Commander (Lieutenant Sato Masao)
  Zuiho Carrier Fighter Unit 19 (18) Type 0
  Zuiho Carrier Attack Unit 6 (6) Type 97
Heavy cruiser: *Kumano*
Destroyers (from Destroyer Divisions 4 and 16): *Amatsukaze, Hatsukaze, Tokitsukaze, Yukikaze, Arashi, Maikaze, Teruzuki, Hamakaze*

Vanguard Force (Rear Admiral Abe Hiroaki in *Hiei*)
Battleship Division 11
  Battleships: *Hiei, Kirishima*
Cruiser Division 7
  Heavy cruiser: *Suzuya*
Cruiser Division 8
  Heavy cruisers: *Chikuma, Tone*
Destroyer Squadron 10
  Light cruiser *Nagara*
  Destroyers from Destroyer Divisions 10 and 17: *Akigumo, Makigumo, Yugumo, Kazegumo, Isokaze, Tanikaze, Urakaze*

UNITED STATES NAVY

Task Force 61 (Rear Admiral Thomas C. Kinkaid)
Task Force 16 (Kinkaid)
Enterprise (Captain Osborne B. Hardison)
  Carrier Air Group 10 (Commander Richard K. Gaines)   1 (1) TBF-1
  Fighting Ten 34 (31) F4F-4
  Bombing Ten 14 (10) SBD-3
  Scouting Ten 20 (13) SBD-3
  Torpedo Ten 9 (9) TBF-1
Battleship: *South Dakota*
Heavy cruiser: *Portland*
Light cruiser: *San Juan*
Destroyer Squadron 5
  Destroyers: *Porter, Mahan, Cushing, Preston, Smith, Maury, Conyngham, Shaw*

Task Force 17 (Rear Admiral George D. Murray)
Hornet (Captain Charles P. Mason)
  Hornet Air Group (Commander Walter F. Rodee) 1 (1) TBF-1
  Fighting Seventy-Two 38 (33) F4F-4
  Bombing Eight 15 (14) SBD-3
  Scouting Eight 16 (10) SBD-3
  Torpedo Six 15 (15) TBF-1
Heavy cruisers: *Northampton, Pensacola*
Light cruisers: *San Diego, Juneau*
Destroyer Squadron 2
  Destroyers: *Morris, Anderson, Hughes, Mustin, Russell, Barton*

Task Force 64 (Rear Admiral Willis A. Lee)
Battleship: *Washington*
Heavy cruiser: *San Francisco*
Light cruisers: *Helena, Atlanta*
Destroyers: *Aaron Ward, Benham, Fletcher, Lansdowne, Lardner, McCalla*

OPPOSING PLANS

THE US PLAN

On August 11, Ghormley gave Fletcher his tasks in the aftermath of the successful landing. In addition to his primary mission of defeating the Japanese carrier force should it appear, Fletcher had to cover the Espiritu Santo–Noumea line of communications, support Guadalcanal and Tulagi against Japanese naval attack, and cover the movement of American supplies and reinforcements to the islands. After the battle of Savo Island, the Japanese were in undisputed control of the waters around Guadalcanal at night and even running supplies into Guadalcanal during the day required a major operation with carrier support.

The dilemma for Fletcher was that he had to remain close to Guadalcanal to intercept a major Japanese operation against the Marines. This was driven by the fact that long-range search assets operating out of Espiritu Santo could not be counted on to provide the required advance warning of a Japanese move against Guadalcanal. Fletcher adopted a tactic of operating in the waters between San Cristobal and Espiritu Santo, but staying out of Japanese air search range. His goal was to be within 12 hours' striking range of Guadalcanal. To accomplish his mission, Fletcher possessed three carriers and a fourth, *Hornet*, departed Pearl Harbor for the South Pacific on August 17. The carriers flew twice-daily reconnaissance missions, but Fletcher was dependent upon the long-range searches from Catalina flying boats to provide him with warning. In addition, he expected strategic warning of major Japanese operations from American intelligence. This is how the battle of the Eastern Solomons took shape. When Catalinas detected Japanese fleet movements and a reinforcement convoy heading toward Guadalcanal, Fletcher moved his carriers north to intervene.

Halsey's plan at Santa Cruz

When Halsey took over from Ghormley, he immediately decided to go on the offensive. His first concern was how to relieve the threat to the Marines on Guadalcanal. For naval forces, Halsey's principal assets were two carriers and two modern battleships. Within days of assuming command, Halsey and his staff developed a bold plan to use all available naval forces. The centerpiece was TF-61, which would again include two carriers on October 24 when *Enterprise* arrived in the area and rendezvoused with *Hornet* northeast of the New Hebrides. The following day, TF-61 was to move north of the Santa

American and Japanese bases in the South Pacific, September–October 1942

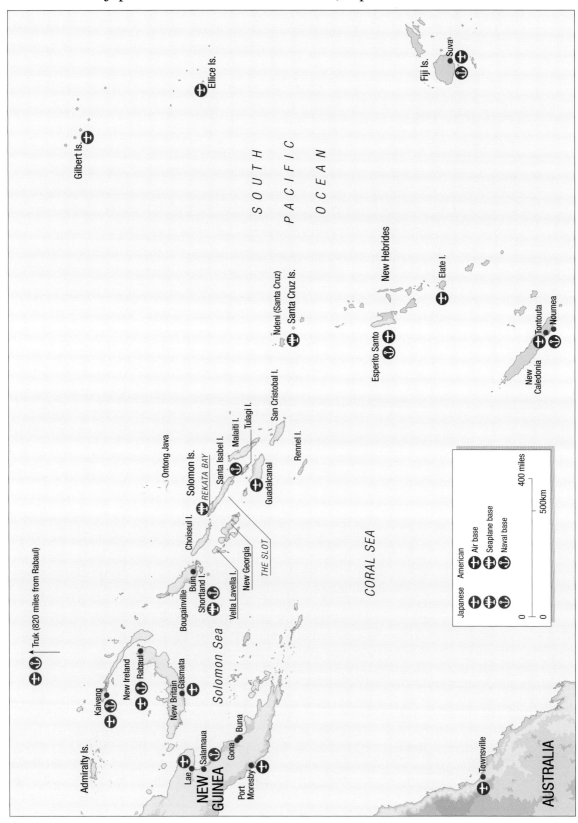

Fiji Is.
Suva

Ellice Is.

Gilbert Is.

S O U T H   P A C I F I C   O C E A N

New Hebrides

Elate I.

Ndeni (Santa Cruz)
Santa Cruz Is.

Esperito Santo

Tontouta
Noumea
New Caledonia

Malaiti I.
Tulagi I.
San Cristobal I.

Rennel I.

Ontong Java

Solomon Is.
Santa Isabel I.
REKATA BAY

Guadalcanal

Choiseul I.

THE SLOT

New Georgia

Vella Lavella I.

Bougainville
Shortland I.
Buin

Truk (820 miles from Rabaul)

New Ireland
Rabaul
Kaiveng
New Britain
Gasmata

CORAL SEA

Solomon Sea

Admiralty Is.

Lae
NEW GUINEA
Salamaua
Gona
Buna
Port Moresby

Townsville

AUSTRALIA

	American		
	Air base	Seaplane base	Naval base
Japanese			

0   400 miles
0   500km

36

Cruz Islands. This would place the Americans at the edge of the range of land-based air support from Espiritu Santo, so Halsey ordered the carriers to search aggressively for Japanese forces. If nothing was encountered, TF-61 was to continue toward San Cristobal Island. The next step of the plan was dependent upon Japanese actions. If TF-61's searches revealed no major operations against Guadalcanal, Halsey intended to mount a major spoiling attack against Japanese forces in the Solomons. This would include a strike by his carriers against Japanese shipping off southern Bougainville in the Shortland Islands anchorage which was the major Japanese staging area for reinforcement runs down the "Slot" to Guadalcanal. Halsey even considered committing TF-64 which was being held southeast of Guadalcanal with the battleship *Washington* and several cruisers to bombard the harbor.

After the battle, Halsey stated to Nimitz that he intended TF-61 to proceed past Santa Cruz only if no Japanese forces were in the area. It does not appear that this important element was understood by Kinkaid. Regardless of the true intent of Halsey's plans, they were extremely aggressive, and certainly could be construed as risky. Halsey was committing both of his operational carriers, in fact, the only two operational carriers in the entire Pacific, to an operation where support from land-based air cover was limited. This was in spite of the fact that Halsey had only a vague notion of the location and intention of the Japanese carrier force. Such an operation risked much and stood to gain little. If both of the carriers were lost or severely damaged, Halsey's ability to provide naval support to the Marines on Guadalcanal would be crippled. The more prudent plan would have been for Halsey to maintain his carriers in a position south or southeast of Guadalcanal, relying on the advantage of searches performed by long-ranged Catalinas and B-17s to give him warning of a major Japanese move against Guadalcanal. This was the conservative course of action practiced by Fletcher for the first period of the campaign, but it was not Halsey's style.

His notion of mounting a spoiling attack against shipping in the Shortland Islands was also imprudent given the risks and benefits. The same operation was conducted by *Hornet* alone on October 5, but it resulted in little damage to the Japanese. Assumedly, the Japanese would be more alert the next time and such an operation would place the carriers well within striking range of the land-based aircraft from Rabaul. With the Japanese carriers unlocated, the possibility existed of placing TF-61 between two significant threats. The fact that TF-61 would have to provide defensive air cover to any American surface force ordered to bombard the target, while still providing for its own defense, was totally unrealistic.

Halsey's plan was based on incomplete intelligence. Nimitz's intelligence staff assessed only Carrier Division 1 to be in the South Pacific. Just before the battle, the Office of Naval Intelligence in Washington assessed as many as four carriers as possibly active in the South Pacific. If true, TF-61 would be outnumbered, but Halsey did not change his plan for an aggressive sweep north of the Santa Cruz Islands.

THE JAPANESE PLAN

For his first attempt to engage and destroy the American fleet, Yamamoto committed Carrier Division 1. However, instead of *Zuiho*, *Ryujo* took her place. Carrier Division 2 would take another month to be ready. Overall

Japanese planning was based on a faulty assumption that the American invasion of Guadalcanal was merely a raid. Yamamoto's operation had two primary objectives. The foremost was the destruction of the American fleet. The secondary objective was to move a reinforcement convoy to the island. This consisted of three ships and carried only 1,500 troops. To support the convoy, aircraft from Rabaul would strike Henderson Field with daily attacks and cruisers from Rabaul would bombard the airfield nightly.

As usual, the Japanese plan was complex. In addition to the Kido Butai, Nagumo created a detached carrier group to strike Henderson Field. Supporting the carriers, and in accordance with the new Japanese doctrine, was the Vanguard Force and the Support Force.

Yamamoto's plans at Santa Cruz

For the October operation, Yamamoto committed the largest force yet. The entire operation was predicated on the capture of Henderson Field by troops of the Japanese Seventeenth Army on Guadalcanal. The decisive ground attack was to be launched by forces of the 2nd Division on the night of October 22. However, the attack plan required the 2nd Division to march through heavy jungle to a point south of Henderson Field.

Given the continued Japanese underestimation of the number of defenders on the island, both the IJA and Yamamoto assumed the successful capture of the airfield was all but assured. Once Yamamoto received the word that the airfield was under Japanese control, the Combined Fleet would swing into action. Japanese forces would move south to destroy American naval forces supporting the Marines. This was the mission of the Support Force under Kondo which would be operating north of the Solomons beyond the range of American air searches. Kondo's forces included the Advance Force under his direct command and Nagumo's Main Body. As per the new doctrine, the Advance Force would operate 100–120 miles in advance of Nagumo's carriers. The Advance Force also included a carrier component of its own composed of Carrier Division 2. Additionally, Kondo's force included two battleships, four heavy cruisers, a light cruiser and nine destroyers. If all went according to plan, the Advance Force would transit east of Malaita Island and then move into the area of Guadalcanal to mop up any American forces there.

The Main Body was built around Carrier Division 1 with heavy carriers *Shokaku* and *Zuikaku*, and the light carrier *Zuiho*. The carriers were screened by a heavy cruiser and eight destroyers. The remainder of Nagumo's force was formed into the Vanguard Force with two battleships, three heavy cruisers, a light cruiser and seven destroyers. As Kondo moved south toward Guadalcanal, Nagumo would cover his left flank until the Advance Force reached a final position southeast of Guadalcanal.

THE CAMPAIGN

THE BATTLE OF THE EASTERN SOLOMONS

By mid-August, Yamamoto began to assemble a force to move against the American lodgment on Guadalcanal. Since it was assumed that the land offensive would easily rout the Marines and retake the airfield, Yamamoto's first objective was to destroy the American fleet. A small reinforcement convoy was included in the operation with the mission of landing 1,500 men on the island. Nagumo's carriers departed Kure in Japan's Inland Sea on August 16.

On August 20, Japanese flying boats spotted the escort carrier *Long Island* and a fleet carrier 250 miles southeast of Guadalcanal. This and subsequent reports of American aircraft operating from the island (ferried there by the escort carrier) begged the question of how the Japanese would provide air cover for the convoy. The Combined Fleet did not want to use Nagumo's carriers to provide cover since this could disclose their presence to the Americans. The solution reached was not ideal – if the American carriers had not been spotted by August 23, the Japanese carriers would neutralize the airfield on the following day.

Meanwhile, Fletcher was operating in the waters some 300 miles southeast of Guadalcanal. On August 23, American PBY Catalina aircraft spotted the Japanese transport force; upon hearing this, Nagumo turned his carriers to the north to avoid detection. He planned to run north during the night until turning to the southeast on the morning of the 24th. The PBY sighting of the transports at 0950hrs approximately 250 miles north of Guadalcanal, prompted Fletcher to order *Saratoga* to launch a strike of 31 dive-bombers and six torpedo bombers. In the meantime though, the convoy had turned north, and, after running into bad weather, the American strike was unable to locate its target. It was forced to recover on Guadalcanal after dark. A small strike launched from Guadalcanal with nine dive-bombers and 12 fighters also failed to find the convoy.

Fletcher received updated intelligence that evening that the Japanese carriers were at Truk, but not headed to Guadalcanal. Based on this, and the fact that his scouts had found no carriers during the day, Fletcher dispatched the *Wasp* task force (TF-18) south to refuel. This meant she would miss the battle. Fletcher was still confident that the two carriers remaining (*Saratoga* and *Enterprise*) would be more than adequate to prevent the convoy from reaching Guadalcanal.

Nagumo headed north for the remainder of August 23 to remain out of American search range. Instead of deploying some 110–150 miles in front of the carriers as per the new doctrine, Kondo's Advance Force was deployed to the east of the carriers reflecting concern that the American carriers were operating in that direction. The bulk of Nagumo's escorts (known as the Vanguard Force) – two battleships, three heavy and a light cruiser and three destroyers – were deployed only 6 miles ahead of the carriers. At 0400hrs on August 24, Nagumo's force was weakened with the detachment of the light carrier *Ryujo*, heavy cruiser *Tone* and two destroyers to transit to the south in order to be in position to conduct the strike on Henderson Field. Since this was in accordance with an order from Yamamoto to neutralize the airfield, it was not, as is commonly believed, a gambit to draw the attention of the American carriers from the main Japanese carrier force.

Reconnaissance is a key ingredient for success in a carrier battle, but search aircraft neither from American nor Japanese carriers had success on the morning of August 24. American PBYs did spot the *Ryujo* group at 0935hrs, which Fletcher learned of shortly thereafter at 0947hrs. Fletcher declined to mount an immediate strike on the light carrier, instead deciding to wait for word of the fleet carriers. At 1105hrs, the *Saratoga* strike group returned to its ship from Guadalcanal.

Though PBYs found parts of the Advance and Vanguard Forces, Nagumo's fleet carriers were not detected. At 1239hrs, *Enterprise* launched 23 aircraft to conduct searches to the northwest and northeast. About the same time, two Japanese search aircraft were destroyed in close proximity to the American carriers, and Fletcher assumed he had been spotted.

Just after noon, *Ryujo* launched a strike of six carrier attack planes and 15 fighters to hit Henderson Field. The strike ended badly for the Japanese with three fighters and four carrier attack planes destroyed for three Wildcats shot down. By the time the surviving aircraft returned to *Ryujo*, she was no more.

A 550-pound Japanese bomb explodes alongside *Enterprise*. Of the 15 *Shokaku* and three *Zuikaku* dive-bombers which attacked the carrier, only three scored hits and these inflicted only moderate damage. (Naval History and Heritage Command)

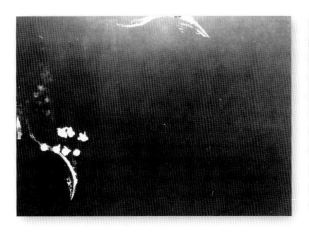

The Japanese got their first major break of the battle when a scout aircraft from heavy cruiser *Chikuma* spotted the American carriers at 1400hrs. By 1455hrs, the first strike group of 18 carrier bombers and four fighters from *Shokaku* and nine carrier bombers and six fighters from *Zuikaku* was headed south. At 1600hrs, another group of 18 carrier bombers and six fighters from *Zuikaku* and another nine carrier bombers and three fighters from *Shokaku* was also in the air. Nagumo had committed 73 aircraft in all.

After some initial hesitation, and with no information available on Nagumo's main carrier force, Fletcher decided to launch a strike from *Saratoga* of 29 Dauntlesses (after one abort) and seven Avengers (after another abort) against *Ryujo* at about 1340hrs. After this decision, reports began to filter in from *Enterprise*'s scouts. At 1410hrs, *Ryujo* was located; at 1440hrs, Dauntlesses spotted the Advance Force and bombed the heavy cruiser *Maya*. Most importantly, at 1500hrs, *Saratoga* received a post attack report by two *Enterprise* dive-bombers which had just unsuccessfully attacked *Shokaku*.

This development put Fletcher in an unenviable position. His main strike was en route to strike a secondary target, and now he had information on the location of the main Japanese carrier force. At 1550hrs, the attack by *Saratoga*'s strike group began. After successfully dodging the first ten or so bombs, *Ryujo* was struck by as many as three bombs and a torpedo hit starboard. She later sank at 2000hrs with the loss of 121 crewmen. The surviving aircraft from the Guadalcanal strike and her CAP fighters were forced to ditch alongside the destroyers and their aircrew rescued.

The Japanese riposte was not long in coming. At 1602hrs, *Enterprise*'s radar gained first contact on a large group of aircraft 88 miles to the northwest. Between his two carriers, Fletcher had 53 fighters on CAP.

The Japanese flight commander split his 27 dive-bombers into two groups and approached his target from the north at 16,000ft. This placed most of the defending fighters at the tactical disadvantage of being below the Japanese. The fighter direction circuit was quickly disabled with unnecessary transmissions, which made effective control impossible. All 53 fighters, their controller onboard *Enterprise*, and the returning reconnaissance aircraft were all on the same narrow frequency. Of the 53 Wildcats, only as many as seven were in position to attack the nine *Zuikaku* dive-bombers before they dove on their target and another ten Wildcats engaged the Japanese dive-bombers on their way down to the target. The Japanese intended to split their attack, with 18 dive-bombers attacking *Enterprise* and the other nine targeted

LEFT
Just after 1800hrs, three B-17s from Espiritu Santo attacked the crippled *Ryujo*. No hits were scored, as is evident in this photo. Two destroyers are under way near the carrier and heavy cruiser *Tone* is visible at the top of the photo. (Naval History and Heritage Command)

RIGHT
A Type 99 carrier bomber shot down directly over *Enterprise* on August 24. Only eight of the 27 dive-bombers that attacked TF-16 during the battle returned to their carriers. (Naval History and Heritage Command)

against *Saratoga*, but in the aftermath of the confusing air battle all surviving dive-bombers attacked *Enterprise*.

The first bomb hit on *Enterprise* was scored at 1644hrs near the number three elevator where it penetrated several decks and exploded in a messroom killing 35 men. A second bomb exploded just seconds later within feet of the first hit, killing another 35 men. The third and final hit struck near the number two elevator but was only a low order detonation. At least seven dive-bombers attempted to bomb the battleship *North Carolina* trailing 2,500ft behind the carrier. No hits were scored on the battleship, but a couple of near misses caused superficial damage.

The attack cost the Japanese 17 dive-bombers and three Zeros; one other carrier bomber and three Zeros were forced to ditch before returning to their carriers. The Americans lost eight defending Wildcats. The *Enterprise* was wounded, but not seriously; personnel losses were significant with 75 dead and 95 wounded. Within an hour she was able to steam at 24 knots and recover aircraft.

The second Japanese strike seemed poised to finish off the wounded carrier after *Enterprise* suffered a steering casualty at 1821hrs which caused her to reduce speed and circle helplessly. Steering was not repaired until 1858hrs. In this time, the second Japanese strike group passed 50 miles south of *Enterprise* before turning northwest and then departing the area. This was possibly the last chance the Japanese had to finish off *Enterprise* since Nagumo decided not to launch any other strikes.

The American response against the Japanese carrier force was uncoordinated and ineffective. Just before the arrival of the first wave of Japanese attackers, Fletcher ordered all available and ready dive-bombers and torpedo bombers after the Japanese. From *Enterprise*, 11 dive-bombers and seven torpedo bombers took off with orders to attack *Ryujo*. Another two Dauntlesses and five Avengers took off from *Saratoga* with orders to join the *Enterprise* group. The rendezvous never occurred, and none of the *Enterprise* aircraft found a target. The *Saratoga* strike found the Advance Force at 1735hrs and attacked the largest ship present, the seaplane carrier *Chitose*. Two near misses were scored which caused flooding and a list, but the ship survived.

The fate of the Japanese reinforcement convoy was not decided on August 24. Not long after 2300hrs, it turned south again to head to Guadalcanal. The next day, the convoy was subjected to attack by dive-bombers from

Guadalcanal. A light cruiser and one of the three transports were hit. Later that morning, B-17s from Espiritu Santo sank a destroyer alongside the now motionless transport. This was enough for Yamamoto who ordered the cancellation of the transport operation.

The third carrier clash of the war ended indecisively, but, overall, the battle of the Eastern Solomons was an American victory. The Japanese attempt to land reinforcements on Guadalcanal was thwarted and they had failed to destroy the American carriers. Japanese losses were higher with light carrier *Ryujo*, a destroyer and a transport sunk and 75 aircraft lost. The Americans lost a total of 25 aircraft and *Enterprise* was damaged enough to force her to return to Pearl Harbor for repairs.

The Americans could not have been satisfied with their performance. Mounting coordinated air strikes had again proved difficult. The Americans were fortunate that a communications failure had failed to vector the second Japanese strike onto the wounded *Enterprise*. Fighter direction continued to be a problem with only a third of the fighters committed to CAP being able to engage the enemy. There were still difficulties in conducting air searches and getting the information to the right command authority in a timely manner.

The Japanese also had cause for concern. They had done a good job with their air searches but when the critical moment came, the second attack wave received incorrect information that cost them a chance to finish off *Enterprise*. On a larger level, the battle showed the difficulty of fighting the primary threat of American carriers while still facing an unneutralized Henderson Field. This dilemma would persist into the next carrier battle. Heavy losses in aircrew were also a concern and continued the steady attrition of the highly trained prewar aircrew.

Following the Eastern Solomons, *Enterprise* was dispatched for Pearl Harbor on September 3 and arrived a week later going immediately into dry dock for repairs. On August 27, *Saratoga* and *Wasp* returned to the waters between San Cristobal and Santa Cruz. The same day, Ghormley issued new guidance to Fletcher. Concerned that the Japanese carriers could attempt to

Chitose in 1938. The Japanese Navy was alone in developing large seaplane carriers which carried a relatively large number of aircraft and several catapults. Once launched, the aircraft had to land in the water alongside the ship or recover at a land base. *Chitose* and her sister ship were later converted into light carriers with a conventional flight deck. (Yamato Museum)

The battle of the Eastern Solomons, August 24, 1942

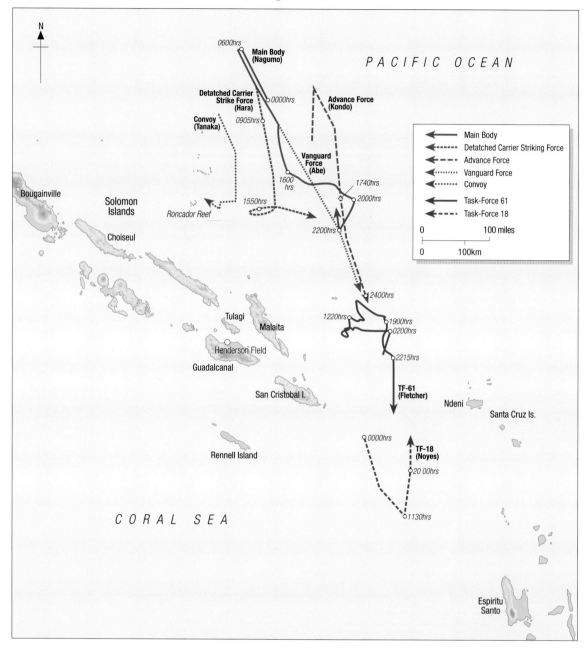

strike targets on Espiritu Santo, or even on Fiji and Samoa, he wanted his carriers positioned farther to the east to respond to this potential threat, while still being within supporting range of Guadalcanal. The new orders kept Fletcher further south of Guadalcanal unless an important target required him to move north. Fletcher received a replacement for *Enterprise* when *Hornet* rendezvoused with TF-61 on August 29.

Fletcher continued his pattern of running north during the night to be within strike range of Guadalcanal in the morning, then heading south during the day to remain out of range of Japanese search aircraft. This operational pattern was taking place in sub-infested waters and it was not difficult to predict

eventual trouble. Early on August 31, the inevitable happened when fleet submarine *I-26* succeeded in putting a torpedo into the slow-to-maneuver *Saratoga*. The single torpedo hit at 0748hrs brought her to a temporary halt and resulted in flooding. The damage to *Saratoga* had several important implications. Not only were the Americans now reduced to two operational carriers in the South Pacific (*Wasp* and *Hornet*), but the aircraft from the damaged carrier ended up on Guadalcanal greatly increasing the defensive and offensive power of Henderson Field. *Saratoga* arrived at Pearl Harbor on August 21 with Fletcher onboard. Fletcher left Oahu on September 27 for the US and never returned to the South Pacific.

Ghormley was still concerned about a Japanese attempt to strike against the sea lines of communications to Australia. On September 3, he ordered TF-61 to move another 120 miles to the south and farther to the east to protect the Fijis and Samoa and to keep them out of waters known to contain Japanese submarines. This took the carriers out of direct support range of Guadalcanal, but they would return if suitable targets presented themselves. Rear Admiral Leigh Noyes took over command of TF-61.

On September 9, the Kido Butai with carriers *Shokaku*, *Zuikaku* and *Zuiho* departed Truk to support the latest Japanese land attempt to seize Henderson Field. Yamamoto planned for Kondo's Support Force (composed of the Advance Force and Nagumo's carriers) to move south to eliminate the American carriers after the airfield had been captured. The Japanese carrier

This is a view of *Enterprise*'s starboard quarter 5in./38 gun battery after the explosion of a 532-pound high-explosive bomb. The bomb hit near the deck edge and the resulting flames engulfed the gun gallery which killed all 38 men of the gun crews and set off the ready 5in. ammunition lockers. (Naval History and Heritage Command)

Wasp afire and sinking after being torpedoed by Japanese submarine *I-19* south of San Cristobal Island on September 15. With her loss, *Hornet* became the only operational carrier in the South Pacific. (Naval History and Heritage Command)

air groups would not be committed to help neutralize Henderson Field – that was a job for the land-based aircraft operating from Rabaul. The carrier aircraft had to be preserved for the anticipated carrier battle.

The Japanese ground offensive climaxed on the night of September 13, but was repulsed with heavy losses. During the offensive, the carriers *Wasp* and *Hornet* assumed a position northeast of the Santa Cruz Islands. American searches were unable to find the Japanese carriers which were also at sea. Japanese searches did locate TF-61, but Noyes moved it to the southeast before the Japanese could close the contact. The next day, PBYs spotted Kondo's Advance Force and Noyes decided to attack, launching strikes from both his carriers. Yamamoto had ordered Kondo's force to head north to refuel, so it was not spotted by the American strike. Had the American strike found and struck the Advance Force, Nagumo would have headed south to support Kondo, and a full carrier battle would have been set up for September 15.

Instead, the next day brought disaster for the Americans. While conducting routine flight operations, TF-61 blundered into a scouting line of Japanese submarines. One of these, *I-19*, fired a full salvo of six torpedoes. Two torpedoes struck *Wasp* with immediate and fatal effect. Fires erupted and subsequent gasoline vapor explosions doomed the ship. The ship was abandoned at about 1420hrs and later sank at 2000hrs. While the loss of *Wasp* was bad enough, the remaining torpedoes continued to the northeast toward TF-17 and *Hornet* some 7 miles away. One hit the battleship *North Carolina* and created a 32 by 15ft hole on her port bow, and another hit the destroyer *O'Brien*. The battleship survived though it was forced to Pearl Harbor for repairs, but the destroyer sank on her way to Pearl Harbor. It was the single most deadly torpedo salvo of the war. It also reduced the Americans to a single operational carrier in the Pacific. The Japanese had five, and three were positioned at Truk.

THE BATTLE OF SANTA CRUZ

After two failed attempts to dislodge the Marines, Yamamoto changed his strategic focus from destroying the American fleet to supporting the land offensive to seize Henderson Field. He devised a combined sea and air operation to neutralize the airfield, thus allowing sufficient ground forces to be landed to seize the airfield successfully. After that had been accomplished, the Combined Fleet would close on Guadalcanal to destroy the American fleet as it rushed to the aid of the Marines.

On October 11, Yamamoto put his plan in motion. Two large seaplane carriers departed Shortland Island bound for Guadalcanal carrying heavy ground equipment. Supporting these was a force of three heavy cruisers and two destroyers tasked to bombard Henderson Field in the early hours of October 12. Also on this day, the Advance Force and the Main Body departed Truk. Yamamoto intensified land-based air attacks on Henderson Field with two-a-day attacks beginning on October 11. Late on the night of October 11, an American task force intercepted the Japanese cruiser force tasked to bombard Henderson Field. The resulting engagement, known as the battle of Cape Esperance, was the first American victory in a night battle during the campaign. The Japanese lost a heavy cruiser and a destroyer sunk, but the reinforcement group completed its mission.

As the Japanese offensive was put into motion, Ghormley had only a single operational carrier. On October 12, Japanese search aircraft spotted *Hornet* operating west of Rennell Island. The carrier was covering a convoy which moved the US Army's 164th Infantry Regiment to Guadalcanal on October 13. Yamamoto also planned a large reinforcement convoy to Guadalcanal with six transports and eight destroyers. Onboard were seven infantry battalions and heavy weapons. To support the movement of the convoy, Yamamoto played a new card. On the night of October 13–14, two battleships bombarded Henderson Field with 918 14in. rounds destroying 40 aircraft and putting the airfield temporarily out of commission. The Japanese convoy arrived on the island on the night of October 14–15, proceeded by two heavy cruisers again shelling the airfield. Aircraft from carriers *Junyo* and *Hiyo* flew air cover over the transports. American aircraft from Henderson Field did succeed in sinking three of the six transports, but not until 4,500 men had been landed along with two-thirds of their supplies and equipment. Yamamoto kept up the pressure with another cruiser bombardment on the night of October 15–16 and more reinforcement destroyer runs.

The Japanese failed to find *Hornet* on October 15; the next day, *Hornet* closed to within 95 miles of Guadalcanal and launched four strikes against the beached Japanese transports. On October 17, Yamamoto ordered Carrier Division 2 to attack shipping in the Lunga anchorage. Kakuta launched 18 fighters and 18 carrier attack planes armed with bombs. They unsuccessfully attacked two destroyers off Guadalcanal and suffered heavily in return. Of the 18 carrier attack planes, only eight returned.

Heading into the next round of combat, Ghormley was pessimistic about whether Guadalcanal could be held. On October 15, he sent a message to Nimitz describing his forces as "totally inadequate" to meet the next Japanese offensive. When Nimitz had visited the South Pacific from September 30 to October 2, he found pessimism in control at Ghormley's headquarters at Noumea, but that the commanders on Guadalcanal were confident they could hold if supported.

Halsey confers with Major General Alexander Vandegrift, commander of the 1st Marine Division on Guadalcanal. Halsey was determined to support Vandegrift with all available means, prompting his decision to use his carriers aggressively at Santa Cruz. (Naval History and Heritage Command)

Nimitz made the choice, approved by King, to replace Ghormley with Halsey who had departed Hawaii on October 14 to conduct an inspection of the South Pacific before assuming command of TF-16 and then taking over as commander of TF-61. Halsey's assignment as Commander, South Pacific was undoubtedly the right move at the right time. The assignment of the aggressive Halsey indicated that Nimitz would do everything he could to support the Marines on Guadalcanal. With Halsey in charge, the American forces would be handled much more aggressively in the upcoming October battles.

Halsey's new assignment meant another shuffling of the American carrier commanders. Kinkaid retained command of TF-16 built around *Enterprise*, now returned from Hawaii after repair, and Murray remained in command of TF-17 built around *Hornet*. Since Kinkaid was senior, he assumed command of TF-61 as senior task force commander. The American situation by mid-October was serious. Attrition to the aircraft on Henderson Field was high and there were relatively few replacements in the Pacific that could be allocated to Guadalcanal. The role of Halsey's two carriers was key.

On October 21, an engine room fire broke out on *Hiyo*. Repairs by her crew brought her speed back up to 16 knots, but this was insufficient for the carrier to continue operations. The next day, Kakuta sent the carrier to Truk with two destroyers. Before departing, *Hiyo* transferred three fighters, one carrier bomber and five carrier attack planes to *Junyo*. Nevertheless, the departure of *Hiyo* took 16 fighters and 17 carrier bombers out of the battle.

Problems getting forces into their pre-attack positions forced the Seventeenth Army to delay the attack on Henderson Field from the night of October 22 to the next night. This forced the Support Force to recalibrate its movements in order not to be discovered prematurely. Yamamoto ordered Kondo to move north until noon on the 22nd before again turning south. At midday, according to the new timeline, the Support Force again headed south.

With the attack scheduled for the night of October 23, the airfield would be in Japanese hands the next morning. At this time, the Advance Force was planned to be 200 miles northeast of Henderson Field with the Japanese carriers another 100 miles behind.

Japanese searches were unsuccessful on October 23, but American PBYs spotted Nagumo's Vanguard Force and one of his carriers. Halsey was now aware that strong Japanese forces were in the area. Nevertheless, he did not change his plan to send his two carriers north of the Santa Cruz Islands.

Owing to continuing problems getting the battalions of the 2nd Division into position south of Henderson Field, the IJA again delayed the start of the attack until the night of October 24. This forced the entire Support Force to head north again. Yamamoto again planned to have the Support Force in position north of Guadalcanal on the morning of the 25th after the expected capture of the airfield. He remained concerned about the lack of information about American carriers. Japanese air searches did reveal the movements of TF-64 (built around the battleship *Washington*) southeast of Guadalcanal as it headed back to Espiritu Santo, making Yamamoto wonder whether it was being used as bait to lure Japanese forces to the south, exposing their flank to the American carriers suspected to be operating to the east. Yamamoto warned Kondo and Nagumo to search for the American carriers which he suspected to be to the southeast of the Support Force.

After refueling at Espiritu Santo, TF-64 departed on October 23. The commander of the Marines on Guadalcanal flew to Noumea to meet with Halsey that same day. Halsey promised him he would do everything possible to support his Marines. He soon made good his promise.

On October 24, *Enterprise* rendezvoused with *Hornet* 250 miles northeast of Espiritu Santo. Kinkaid now took command of the reestablished TF-61. He decided to keep each carrier in its own formation and ordered TF-17 to operate 5 miles to the southeast of his flagship. In accordance with Halsey's plan, Kinkaid ordered TF-61 to make 23 knots and move to the waters north of Santa Cruz.

Events on October 24 greatly disturbed Nagumo. American PBYs delivered an unsuccessful attack on his Vanguard Force during the early morning hours. This attack, and the fact that the Japanese carriers had been spotted the day before, created uncertainty and caution in Nagumo. At the urging of Kusaka, his chief of staff, Nagumo decided to continue his transit to the north beyond what Yamamoto had ordered. He continued to the northwest until the afternoon of the 24th, and did not even inform Kondo and Yamamoto of his new intent until that afternoon. Meanwhile, Kondo had already turned south according to the overall plan. Upon learning of Nagumo's alteration, Kondo had to conform. This delay did not go down well with Yamamoto. At 2147hrs, he ordered Nagumo and Kondo to get back on schedule. Finally, at 2300hrs on October 24, Nagumo reversed course to the south and increased speed to 26 knots.

The Japanese ground attack finally got started on the night of October 24. The attack was chaotic and was defeated piecemeal by the Marines. In the confusion, at 0130hrs on October 25, the IJA passed the word to Yamamoto that the airfield had been taken. In fact, the airfield remained in American hands. Throughout the day, the Japanese attempted to keep fighters over Henderson Field, including a strike by 12 *Junyo* fighters and 12 carrier bombers from 200 miles north of Henderson at about 1600hrs. The robust American fighter response during the day left no doubt that the airfield was still in operation.

October 25 found both sides groping in the dark. Both Kondo and Nagumo had resumed movement to Guadalcanal late on the 24th. Kondo's Advance Force was in position 120 miles southwest of Nagumo. The elation over the reported capture of Henderson Field was short lived. In response to the news that the airfield remained in American hands, Kondo and Nagumo both headed again to the north.

Throughout the day, long-range American search aircraft did excellent work. PBYs and B-17s from Espiritu Santo and from seaplane tender *Ballard* deployed to the southernmost of the Santa Cruz Islands were active and productive. At 0930hrs, a B-17 spotted the Advance Force. Within minutes, a PBY spotted the Vanguard Force. Another PBY began to shadow Nagumo's Main Body beginning at 1000hrs. By 1103hrs, it had spotted all three of Nagumo's carriers.

News of the PBY contacts reached Kinkaid at 1025hrs. The original report included mention of battleships and escorts, but no carriers. The Japanese were 375 miles to the northwest of TF-61 and this was far out of striking range. *Enterprise* was the duty carrier handling all searches and CAP while *Hornet* maintained a full strike on alert. At 1119hrs a Wildcat with an engine malfunction attempted to recover on *Enterprise*. The pilot forgot to deploy his tailhook, and he smashed through the wire barrier into the Dauntlesses parked forward. The accident destroyed the fighter and four dive-bombers and fouled the deck for an extended period. As the deck crew was clearing things up, *Enterprise* received one of the PBY spotting reports with information on two Japanese carriers. The Japanese were reported to be steaming at 25 knots headed toward TF-61. The contacts were 355 miles to the west of TF-61. As Kinkaid and his staff pondered possible actions, Halsey, who was in receipt of the same information, weighed in with new orders: "Strike, Repeat, Strike."

Tactical factors made this order hard to execute. Kinkaid did not receive the spotting report on the carriers until 1150hrs, and at 355 miles distant from TF-61, the Japanese were well beyond his striking range. Adding to the problem, the wind was coming from the southeast meaning that Kinkaid would have to turn away from the Japanese force to conduct flight operations. This would make it hard for him to close the contact. Kinkaid increased speed to 27 knots to reduce the distance to the reported position. Kinkaid's staff calculated that it would be possible to make an afternoon strike if the Japanese maintained their course and TF-61 continued to close the range. At this point, Kinkaid inexplicably designated *Enterprise*'s inexperienced air group for the afternoon strike instead of using the *Hornet* strike already on alert.

Kinkaid decided to launch an afternoon search of 12 Dauntlesses in six pairs to search to the northwest out to 200 miles. An hour later, *Enterprise* planned to launch a strike of 16 fighters, 12 dive-bombers and seven torpedo bombers to fly 150 miles to the northwest awaiting information from the search aircraft. The operation by the inexperienced *Enterprise* air group did not proceed as planned. The 12 search aircraft took off at about 1330hrs. The launch of the 35-aircraft strike began after 1400hrs, but when the strike departed at 1425hrs, only eight fighters, five dive-bombers and six torpedo planes were in the group. After the departure of the strike, Kinkaid learned at 1510hrs that a group of B-17s had just bombed the Vanguard Force which was headed north at 25 knots. It was now obvious that the airborne strike would never be able to contact the retreating Japanese. Despite Kinkaid's orders that the strike proceed only 150 miles outbound in order to recover before night, the strike commander took his aircraft out to 200 miles and then proceeded to take another 80-mile dog-leg to the north. This made the aircraft short on fuel and required a night recovery. The result was a disaster. One fighter, four dive-bombers and three torpedo planes were lost or damaged beyond repair.

On the night of October 25, both sides took steps that guaranteed that the carrier showdown would occur the next day. Kinkaid's order to move north of the Santa Cruz Islands had not been altered by Halsey. This was the most controversial decision of the battle. Though his original plan called for the sweep north of the Santa Cruz Islands to be executed only in the absence of enemy carriers, Halsey did not cancel the movement now that he had solid information that Nagumo was in the area. Instead of keeping the carriers south of Guadalcanal able to react to direct threats to the Marines, Halsey sent them into an operation at the edge of land-based air support. The reasons for this remain unclear. Halsey was confident, perhaps overconfident, of the capabilities of the American carriers to handle their Japanese counterparts. As he demonstrated throughout the war, he would never pass up an opportunity to engage the Japanese carrier force. He had promised the Marines on Guadalcanal that he would fight, and the Japanese force north of Guadalcanal posed a direct threat to the Marines. All of these factors made Halsey send his carriers into harm's way.

Kinkaid made all preparations for the impending clash. The performance of *Enterprise*'s air group on October 25 was not promising. A total of two fighters, seven dive-bombers, and three torpedo planes had been lost to all causes. This reduced CAG-10's operational air strength to 31 fighters, 23 dive-bombers, and ten torpedo planes. Kinkaid designated *Enterprise* as the duty carrier for October 26 meaning she would handle all search and CAP duties. This kept *Hornet*'s air group as the designated strike group. Together, *Enterprise* and *Hornet* would bring 137 operational aircraft into the battle.

Supporting air operations from Espiritu Santo included an evening PBY sortie for search and five more armed Catalinas departing at 1730hrs. Ten more PBYs and six B-17s were scheduled to depart at 0330hrs on October 26 to re-establish contact with the Japanese.

At 1900hrs, Kondo's Advance Force headed south, followed an hour later by Nagumo's carriers. The Vanguard Force took station 60 miles ahead of the carriers. Yamamoto was tiring of the many delays and, since the Support Force had been at sea since October 11, fuel was becoming an issue. At 2218hrs the Chief of Staff of the Combined Fleet sent a message to Kondo and Nagumo spurring them to greater efforts the next day. Nagumo prepared his three carriers for the next day with initial search, CAP and strike aircraft arrayed on the flight decks and a second strike fueled and armed on the hangar decks. On the three flight decks, and on *Junyo* in the Advance Force, the Japanese brought to bear 194 operational aircraft. In the impending battle, the Japanese would therefore outnumber the Americans in every important category.

THE CARRIERS CLASH

The largest carrier clash of the Guadalcanal campaign was actually initiated by lumbering PBYs. Two of these found elements of Nagumo's fleet. The first sighting report of a Japanese force about 300 miles northwest of TF-61 was

The battle of Santa Cruz, October 26, 1942, 0000–1200hrs

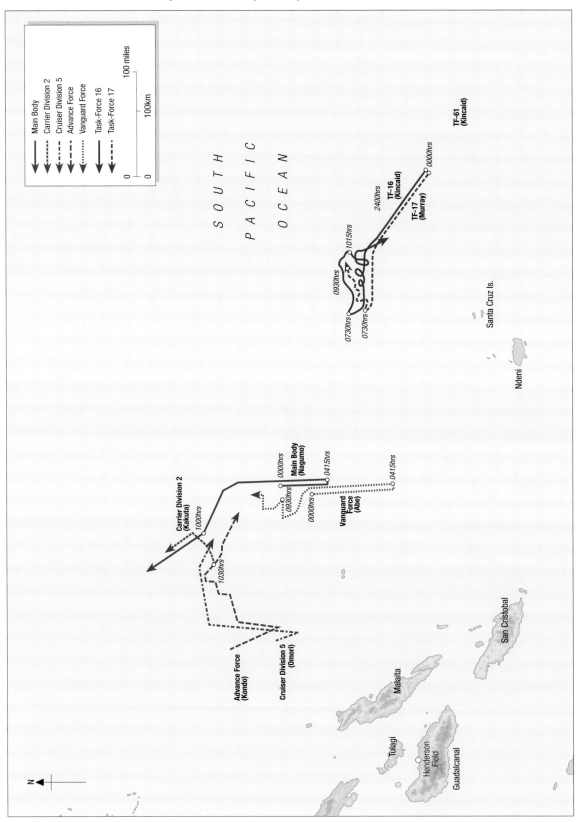

Legend:
- Main Body
- Carrier Division 2
- Cruiser Division 5
- Advance Force
- Vanguard Force
- Task-Force 16
- Task-Force 17

100 miles

100km

SOUTH PACIFIC OCEAN

TF-61 (Kincaid)

0000hrs

TF-16 (Kincaid)

2400hrs

TF-17 (Murray)

1015hrs

0930hrs

0730hrs

0730hrs

Santa Cruz Is.

Ndeni

0000hrs

Main Body (Nagumo)

0415hrs

Carrier Division 2 (Kakuta)

1000hrs

0930hrs

0000hrs

Vanguard Force (Abe)

0415hrs

1030hrs

Advance Force (Kondo)

Cruiser Division 5 (Omori)

San Cristobal

Malaita

Tulagi

Henderson Field

Guadalcanal

N

issued at 0022hrs. Minutes later, the same PBY reported attacking a Japanese "heavy cruiser" with a torpedo. This was actually a destroyer in the Vanguard Force. At 0250hrs, another PBY spotted the carrier *Zuikaku* and executed a glide bombing run to drop its four 500-pound bombs. These landed some 300 yards off the big carrier's starboard side.

These unsuccessful attacks reinforced Nagumo's fears of an ambush by unlocated American carriers he thought to be operating out to his east. In response to the surprise PBY attack, he ordered his force to reverse course to the north at 0330hrs and that all the aircraft on the hangar bay be defueled and de-armed. At 0445hrs, the Japanese launched 14 carrier attack planes to search the sectors from 050 to 230 degrees out to 300 miles. For the search, *Shokaku* and *Zuikaku* each contributed four aircraft and *Zuiho* six. At 0520hrs, *Zuiho* launched the first CAP mission of the day with three fighters. An additional 22 fighters were on deck standby and a total of 70 aircraft were spotted for the first strike. This included 20 aircraft from *Shokaku*'s carrier attack plane squadron and 22 dive-bombers from *Zuikaku*.

Flight deck crews on the American carriers were also busy. At about 0500hrs, TF-61 reversed course from the northwest to the southeast to execute flight operations. *Enterprise* flew off seven fighters for CAP and 16 Dauntlesses to conduct a search in pairs out to 200 miles to the west. At sunrise, *Hornet* added another seven fighters to the overhead CAP.

The potential advantages gained by the night PBY operations were largely wasted by communications problems. These meant that any chance Kinkaid had of attacking the Japanese carriers with their strike aircraft still on deck was wasted. He did not learn of the PBY attack on *Zuikaku* until 0512hrs, though other ships in TF-61 learned of it an hour earlier but did not pass the information to Kinkaid's flagship. Had the information reached him earlier, Kinkaid would not have had to devote 16 dive-bombers to search missions. When his staff learned of the PBY sighting report, they urged Kinkaid to send *Hornet*'s ready aircraft on a search-strike mission. Kinkaid deferred, no doubt because of the previous day's experience which cost him heavily.

Enterprise's scout planes soon ran across the Japanese. At 0617hrs, two Dauntlesses spotted the Vanguard Force 170 miles to the west of TF-61. The Japanese were heading north at 20 knots. After being spotted, Abe increased

Zuiho in October 1942 conducting flight operations. One aircraft has just launched, another is climbing forward of the ship, and the remainder of the launch is spotted aft. During the reorganization of the Kido Butai following Midway, *Zuiho* became a dedicated carrier for fighters. (Yamato Museum)

speed to 30 knots and changed direction heading to the northwest. At 0645hrs, two Dauntlesses attacked heavy cruiser *Tone*. The bombs missed, and one American aircraft was lost to antiaircraft fire.

Also at 0645hrs, another pair of Dauntlesses spotted one of Nagumo's carriers, and by 0700hrs had sighted all three. At 0650hrs, the Japanese finally spotted the intruding American aircraft and launched a total of 17 fighters from *Shokaku* and *Zuikaku*. The CAP was able to thwart an attack by the original pair of Dauntlesses and another pair nearby.

The sighting of the Japanese carriers put them 185–200 miles to the northwest of TF-61. Kinkaid ordered an immediate strike by both carriers. This was already at the edge of his strike range, and to make things more uncertain, the Japanese were headed north and Kinkaid would have to turn away actually to launch the strike. He changed course to the northwest and increased speed to 27 knots to close the range as much as possible.

Hornet, with her strike already spotted on deck, was the first to launch. Eight fighters, 15 Dauntlesses and six torpedo planes were launched between 0732 and 0743hrs. A second wave of eight fighters (only seven proceeded), nine Dauntlesses (armed with 1,000-pound bombs), and ten Avengers (all armed with 500-pound bombs instead of more powerful torpedoes and also including the unarmed air group commander's aircraft) was brought up to the flight deck and launched within ten minutes of the departure of the first group. Each group proceeded separately to the target.

At 0747hrs, *Enterprise* launched 11 fighters for CAP. The launch of her strike was a hurried affair and reflected poor planning. The strike force was nine torpedo planes (only eight launched) and three dive-bombers escorted by eight fighters. Accompanying the strike was the unarmed aircraft of the air group commander. Despite Kinkaid's desire that the carriers strike together, the *Enterprise* aircraft were ordered not to proceed with *Hornet*'s aircraft. The effect was that three different American strike groups proceeded to the attack area independently.

THE JAPANESE RESPOND

While the Americans were preparing their strike, Nagumo received crucial information. One of *Shokaku*'s carrier attack planes spotted an American carrier to the east-south south only 210 miles away. The pilot of the aircraft first made the discovery at 0612hrs, but it took him a while to confirm the presence of carriers, and when he sent the report, he used an incorrect call sign. Nevertheless, when Nagumo received the report at 0658hrs stating that carriers were present, he did not hesitate. He ordered the first attack wave launched immediately. He also sent the single Yokosuka D4Y1-C Type 2 carrier reconnaissance plane (later code-named "Judy" by the Allies) to confirm the sighting. The Japanese strike began its launch at 0710hrs. The strike was under the command of Lieutenant-Commander Murata Shigeharu from *Shokaku*; Murata was the most accomplished torpedo bomber pilot in the IJN and had commanded the 40 torpedo bombers at Pearl Harbor which had laid waste to Battleship Row. From *Shokaku* came four fighters and 20 carrier attack planes with torpedoes. From *Zuikaku*, beginning at 0725hrs, were launched eight fighters, 21 carrier bombers (another was forced to abort) and a carrier attack plane without a torpedo tasked to track the American carrier force. Light carrier *Zuiho* contributed nine fighters and another carrier attack plane serving

A strike poised to launch off *Zuikaku* on May 5, 1942 during the preliminaries of the battle of Coral Sea. Visible are 12 Zeros and 17 Type 99 carrier bombers. The scene on *Zuikaku* on the morning of October 26 with her strike spotted on deck must have been very similar. (Yamato Museum)

as a shadow aircraft. By 0730hrs, Murata headed to the southeast. The total Japanese strike force included 21 fighters, 21 carrier bombers with 550-pound bombs, and 22 carrier attack planes (only 20 carried torpedoes).

After the launch of the first wave, *Shokaku* and *Zuikaku* began the process of moving the second attack wave up from the hangar deck to the flight deck. During this process, at 0740hrs, two Dauntless dive-bombers responding to the original report of Japanese carriers arrived over Nagumo's force and achieved complete surprise. Undetected by the radar on *Shokaku* and unmolested by the 21 Japanese fighters aloft on CAP, the two Dauntlesses picked what they thought was a Shokaku-class carrier and attacked. Both pilots claimed hits with their 500-pound bombs. Despite being chased by fighters for 45 miles, both Dauntlesses escaped, shooting down a Zero in the process. Their remarkable attack was actually against *Zuiho*. A single bomb hit aft started a fire and wrecked her arresting gear. Unable to recover aircraft, *Zuiho* was out of the battle.

The Japanese were fortunate that the surprise attack was not against the two larger carriers preparing to arm and fuel aircraft for launch. To Nagumo, it seemed another disaster like Midway was in the offing. Both carriers began frenzied efforts to get the second-wave aircraft in the air before any further attacks. The aircraft on the hangar deck had been disarmed and defueled during the night after the PBY attack, and now flight deck crews on both carriers worked feverishly to prepare the aircraft for launch. The carrier bomber squadron on *Shokaku* needed less time to prepare than the carrier attack plane squadron on *Zuikaku* where all available personnel were still loading the heavy torpedoes. Nagumo ordered that the *Shokaku* attack group be launched as soon as possible without waiting for the aircraft from *Zuikaku*. The first aircraft took off from *Shokaku* at 0810hrs and by 0818hrs, the strike of five Zero fighters and 20 carrier bombers were headed towards the American carriers. One of the dive-bombers later aborted. *Zuikaku* launched 17 torpedo planes (one without a torpedo to act as a shadow plane) and four fighters following behind the *Shokaku* dive-bombers. The strike departed at 0900hrs.

ATTACK ON *ZUIHO* (pp. 56–57)

The first blow of the battle was delivered by a pair of *Enterprise* Dauntless dive-bombers **(1)** on a search mission. Alerted by the initial report of enemy carriers by another pair of *Enterprise* dive-bombers, Lieutenant Stockton Strong and Ensign Charles Irvine headed southwest to the Japanese carriers and avoided detection by Japanese radar and CAP to dive on what they identified as a Shokaku-class carrier at 0740hrs. The pair gained complete surprise and began their dive from 14,000ft. Their actual target was light carrier *Zuiho*

(2) which was steaming several miles to the port of *Shokaku*. Strong placed his 500-pound bomb on the aft portion of *Zuiho*'s flight deck **(3)**. The two Dauntlesses survived attacks by three *Zuikaku* Zeros **(4)** for 45 miles beyond the Japanese task force and one of the Dauntless rear gunners shot down one of the Zeros. *Zuiho* would survive the resulting fires, but she was out of the battle. *Enterprise*'s commanding officer was so impressed with this feat that he recommended Strong for a Medal of Honor.

In addition to throwing all available strike aircraft at the American carrier force, the Japanese made plans for a surface engagement. Between the Advance Force and the Vanguard Force, the Japanese possessed a considerable advantage in gunnery and torpedo power. These ships could destroy any American ships damaged by air attack. Kondo ordered his Advance Force to increase speed and head to the east-northeast to join with Nagumo. This also closed the range to the reported location of the American carriers so that *Junyo*'s aircraft could launch a strike. Kondo also ordered the Vanguard Force to head to the contact, and by 0925hrs it was also heading east at 26 knots. The Vanguard Force was now operating in two groups; one had the two battleships and a heavy cruiser and a light cruiser and four destroyers, the second comprised cruisers *Tone* and *Chikuma* and two destroyers.

Since the American and Japanese strike groups were headed on reciprocal bearings, many spotted each other heading in opposite directions. One of *Hornet*'s fighters spotted *Shokaku*'s carrier attack planes headed to the southwest at about 0830hrs and radioed a warning to its base but received no acknowledgment. Likewise, *Shokaku*'s strike group saw part of the *Hornet* strike and warned their mother ship.

At about 0835hrs, the escort of the *Shokaku* strike, which included the nine Zero fighters from *Zuiho*, spotted another group of American aircraft. This was the 20-strong *Enterprise* group. The leader of *Zuiho*'s fighters could not resist this target and dove down from 14,000ft to conduct a swift attack to break up the unsuspecting American formation before rejoining Murata's vulnerable carrier attack planes. Coming out of the sun from directly ahead, the Japanese fighters gained complete surprise. In their first pass, the Zeros sent two Avengers into the sea and a third limping home. One of the slashing Zeros was destroyed by the ball turret gunners of the Avengers. Another Zero was shot down by a section of American fighters which belatedly came to the aid of the torpedo bombers, and a third was later destroyed while conducting another attack on the Avengers. The resulting dogfight between the six surviving Zeros and the four Wildcats resulted in another three American fighters shot down and the last forced to return. At the end of the engagement,

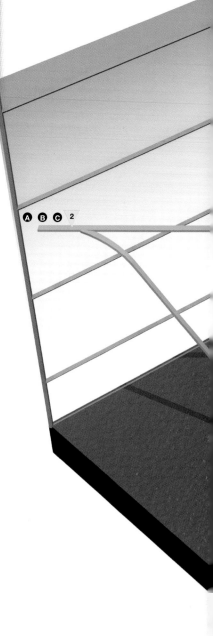

AMERICAN FORCES

Hornet Air Group
A VS-8/VB-8 (15 SBD-3 Dauntlesses)
B VT-6 (6 TBF-1 Avengers)
C VF-72 (8 F4F-4 Wildcats)

JAPANESE FORCES

1 *Shokaku*
2 *Zuikaku*
3 *Zuiho*
4 *Kumano*
5 *Yukikaze*
6 *Amatsukaze*
7 *Maikaze*
8 *Hamakaze*
9 *Teruzuki*
10 *Arashi*
11 *Tokitsukaze*
12 *Hatsukaze*
13 *Zuiho* CAP (4 Type 0 Fighters)
14 *Zuikaku* CAP (7 Type 0) Fighters)
15 *Shokaku* CAP (9 Type 0 Fighters)

EVENTS

1 0850hrs – Twenty Zeros are on CAP over the Main Body. They are deployed near the carriers at various altitudes to defend from both a dive-bombing and a torpedo attack.

2 0910hrs – The *Hornet* strike sights the Vanguard Force and is attacked by three *Zuiho* Zeros which disperse the Wildcat escort and separate the dive-bombers from the torpedo bombers. The six Avengers never sight the Japanese carriers.

3 Approximately 0913hrs – The leader of the *Hornet* dive-bombers, Lieutenant-Commander William Widhelm, spots *Shokaku* and orders an attack.

4 0918–0925hrs – Widhelm's 15 Dauntlesses run a gauntlet of Zeros. Four *Shokaku* Zeros are encountered

first, then two *Zuiho* Zeros. Finally, five *Zuikaku* Zeros join the fray. Four Dauntlesses, including Widhelm's, do not reach the dive point.

5 0927hrs – Ten surviving Dauntlesses reach their pushover point and dive on *Shokaku* from astern. The first three or four 1,000-pound bombs miss the wildly maneuvering carrier, but the next four, and possibly as many as six, hit the ship and cause heavy damage.

6 Approximately 0930hrs – The last Dauntless attacks destroyer *Teruzuki* and misses.

7 Many of the dive-bombers are attacked exiting the area, but none is shot down. Thirteen of 15 Dauntlesses eventually reach TF-61. The Japanese lose two Zeros shot down and another forced to ditch.

AMERICAN CARRIER AIRCRAFT ATTACK *SHOKAKU*

In the first attack of the battle US aircraft critically damage the Japanese carrier.

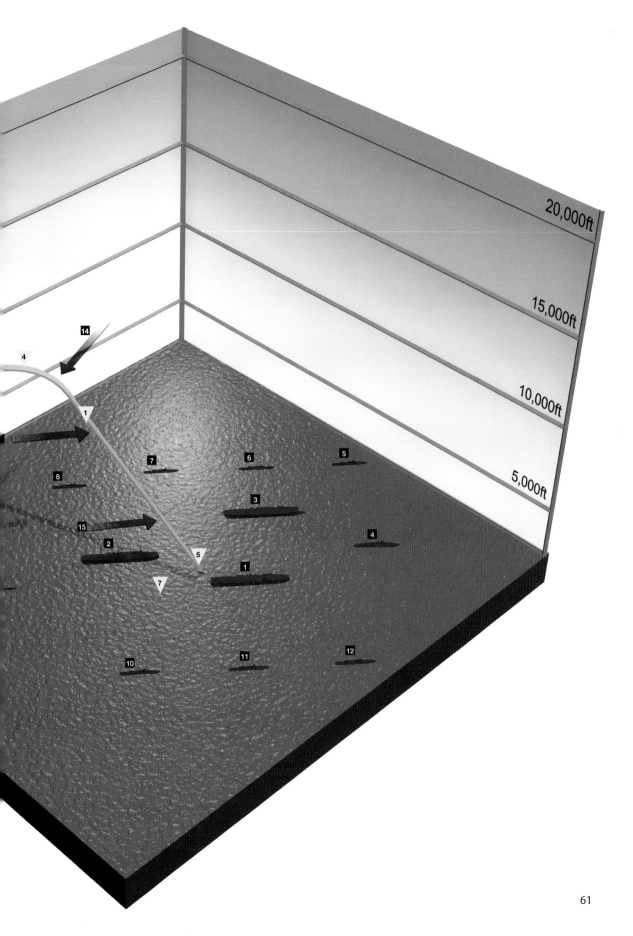

20,000ft

15,000ft

10,000ft

5,000ft

61

the Americans had lost three fighters and two Avengers, with another two Avengers and a fighter forced to return to their carrier. The cost to the Japanese was also high with four Zeros shot down and a fifth heavily damaged.

The effect of this aerial skirmish was major. *Enterprise*'s small strike was reduced to five Avengers (including the carrier air group commander's unarmed aircraft), three Dauntlesses and only four fighters. The five surviving Japanese fighters did not rejoin Murata's torpedo aircraft, but were forced to return to their ship. The decision of the Japanese fighter leader was ill-considered. His mission was to escort the vulnerable torpedo bombers to kill an American carrier, not to engage in a duel with American strike aircraft. The fate of Murata's torpedo bombers proved the foolishness of his decision.

THE AMERICANS ATTACK

At 0840hrs, *Shokaku*'s radar reported a group of American aircraft to the southwest at 78 miles. This was *Hornet*'s first strike group. By this time, 23 Zeros were aloft on CAP. Three had been sent south to cover the Vanguard Force, leaving 20 to defend the carriers. The Japanese deployed them at various altitudes to defend from both a dive-bombing and a torpedo attack. Unlike American fighters which were vectored out some distance from the carrier to meet attacking aircraft as far as possible away from the ship, the Japanese CAP was kept near the carriers. This was probably required because of the inadequate range of the radios installed in the Zeros.

The dive-bombers from *Hornet*'s first wave were the first to attack. At 0850hrs, the strike leader spotted the heavy cruisers *Tone* and *Chikuma* from the Vanguard Force about 150 miles northwest of TF-61. He did not attack, but continued to the northwest where he spotted the rest of the Vanguard Force at about 0910hrs. Over the Vanguard Force, the *Hornet* aircraft were attacked by the three *Zuiho* Zeros covering the Japanese formation. In a single attack, one of the escorting Wildcats was shot down and two others badly damaged and forced to return. In return, a single Zero was shot down. The two remaining Zeros sighted and proceeded to attack the other section of four Wildcats cruising at some 3,000ft above the Avengers. They blasted the leader of the Wildcat section, but lost another Zero. The double ambush by a single section of Zeros stripped all the fighter cover from *Hornet*'s strike. It also separated the 15 Dauntlesses from the six Avengers.

The leader of the *Hornet* dive-bombers, Lieutenant-Commander William Widhelm, commander of VS-8, delivered the most powerful American blow of the battle. In response to the Zero attack over the Vanguard Force, he turned his formation to the right into some clouds. Within minutes, he spotted ships 25 miles ahead which he later confirmed as a large carrier and a smaller one issuing black smoke. This was *Shokaku* and the previously damaged *Zuiho*. *Zuikaku* was under cloud cover and was not spotted. Widhelm unsuccessfully tried to vector on the second wave of *Hornet* aircraft.

After running the gauntlet of Zeros, which accounted for Widhelm's Dauntless and three others, at 0927hrs the ten surviving Dauntlesses reached their pushover point. Below them was *Shokaku* maneuvering wildly and throwing up heavy antiaircraft fire. The dive-bombers attacked from astern, but Captain Arima was successful in avoiding the first three or four of the 1,000-pound bombs. The remaining aircraft inflicted heavy damage scoring at least four and possibly as many as six hits.

Whatever the total number of hits, the damage caused proved calamitous. One bomb hit aft of the island on the starboard side and the rest hit around the center and aft elevators. The flight deck was buckled and the center elevator destroyed. The gun positions on the starboard quarter were destroyed with heavy loss of life. Though the damage was extensive, it was not fatal. There were no aircraft in the hangar bay and the fuel lines had been secured. Only two aircraft were aboard – two carrier attack planes parked on the flight deck. One was consumed by fire but the other positioned on the fantail survived. A large fire was started, but after five hours the damage control teams were able to extinguish it. Most importantly, no damage was suffered below the hangar deck level and the ship was able to maintain full speed. Total casualties were heavy with about 130 killed.

The last Dauntless attacked the destroyer *Teruzuki*. Many of the dive-bombers were damaged exiting the area, but none were shot down. Of the 15 Dauntlesses that attacked, 13 eventually made it back to TF-61. In return, the Japanese lost two Zeros shot down and another forced to ditch.

The six *Hornet* Avengers never saw Nagumo's carriers since they were too far south and west. They missed the turn north by Widhelm and were unable to copy his radio reports of the location of the Japanese carriers. The commander of the six Avengers decided to attack the battleships of the Vanguard Force he had previously flown over.

Escorted by seven Wildcats, nine Dauntlesses and ten Avengers all armed with bombs flew over *Tone* and *Chikuma* at about 0920hrs. This group did not receive Widhelm's reports of the Japanese carrier so was unaware that the Japanese carriers were to the north. With no better targets in sight, the leader of the dive-bombers decided to attack the two cruisers. The actual target selected was *Chikuma* and the attack took only five minutes from 0926 to 0931hrs. One 1,000-pound bomb hit the cruiser on the port side of the bridge at 0926hrs and later in the attack a second bomb hit the starboard side of the forward superstructure. Though heavily damaged, and having suffered serious casualties, the ship was in no danger of sinking.

Chikuma under attack from American carrier aircraft on October 26. The heavy cruiser is at high speed with all her forward 8in. gun turrets trained to port. An aerial recognition mark is on the second turret and both catapults appear to be swung out. Smoke from the bomb hit on the forward superstructure is evident. Despite heavy damage, the ship survived. This shot was taken from Commander Rodee's TBF. (Naval History and Heritage Command)

Hornet's second wave was fragmented. The Avengers and their two remaining Wildcat escorts were attacked by two Zeros, but the Wildcats shot one down and the other withdrew. Eventually, the Avengers turned back the way they came which soon brought them over *Tone* and *Chikuma*. The nine Avengers armed with four 500-pound bombs all selected the unfortunate *Chikuma* for their attacks. The aircraft conducted a glide-bomb approach from astern of the frantically maneuvering cruiser, but results were meager. Five hits were claimed, but only one was confirmed. It hit the starboard torpedo mount aft, starting another fire and destroying a reconnaissance aircraft on the starboard catapult. Total casualties aboard *Chikuma* were 192 dead and 95 wounded from a crew of about 900. One of the Avengers attacked one of the two escorting destroyers after its bombs failed to release on the first run, but missed. No American aircraft were lost.

Just as the Avengers from the second wave arrived over the Japanese cruisers, the six torpedo-armed Avengers from the first wave arrived in the area of the *Tone* and *Chikuma*. These aircraft spotted the same cruisers one hour earlier, and now decided to attack since no other targets were available. The aircraft attacked *Tone* and claimed three torpedo hits. Only five torpedoes were released, and these all missed.

The attack by the *Zuiho* Zeros left the *Enterprise* strike leader with a small group of three Dauntlesses and five Avengers escorted by four Wildcats. Though the *Enterprise* group heard Widhelm's reports of a Japanese carrier, they did not realize that he had turned north instead of proceeding to the northwest. Flying to the northwest, the strike leader soon saw *Tone* and *Chikuma* and later the main body of the Vanguard Group. A search beyond the Vanguard Group turned up nothing, so the *Enterprise* group turned back to attack Abe's force. At 0930hrs, the Avengers attacked the nearest large ship, the heavy cruiser *Suzuya*. The four torpedo bombers came in on the cruiser's port side and on the first run launched two torpedoes, but both missed. Another aircraft conducted a second run to release its torpedo, but it also missed. The final aircraft had to dump its torpedo. The three Dauntlesses from VS-10 became separated from the Avengers. They searched briefly in the area for larger targets, but turned back to attack the *Tone* and *Chikuma* group. At 0939hrs, they attacked *Chikuma* just minutes after *Hornet*'s second-wave Dauntlesses had bombed her. The three *Enterprise* dive-bombers placed two near misses on *Chikuma*'s starboard side which opened a hole and let water into the starboard fireroom, reducing the cruiser's speed.

Kinkaid committed 75 aircraft in the attack on the Japanese carriers, not including the 16 Dauntless scouts sent earlier. The results from this were disappointing. Of the 75 aircraft sent to attack a Japanese flight deck, only ten actually did so and this was almost an accidental result of Widhelm's decision to head to the north. The American attacks suffered from the same problem as in earlier battles – a lack of attack group cohesion. At Santa Cruz, the attacks were conducted in a piecemeal fashion, verging on haphazard. Making this problem worse was an appalling lack of communications. The performance of the Wildcat in its escort role was also ineffective. Japanese CAP performance was much better than at Midway with fighters layered at different altitudes. Better damage control meant that *Shokaku* survived a fearful beating. Direct losses from battle were four Wildcats, two Dauntlesses and two Avengers; many others were forced to ditch. The Japanese lost five fighters from the CAP, one that was later forced to ditch and the four *Zuiho* fighters which decimated the *Enterprise* group.

THE JAPANESE ATTACK

The Americans braced themselves for the Japanese attack they knew was coming. The key to the defense was getting the Wildcats on CAP to intercept the attacking formations well away from the carriers. The *Enterprise* FDO, Lieutenant-Commander John Griffin, was designated as senior FDO for TF-61. Griffin had 11 fighters aloft; he placed seven at 10,000ft over TF-16 and the other four between TF-16 and TF-17. *Hornet*, operating 10 miles to the southwest, had eight fighters at 10,000ft. Griffin placed the Wildcats at 10,000ft to conserve fuel and oxygen, believing that radar would give him plenty of warning to move the fighters higher if required and, remarkably, he was unaware that TF-16 had even been sighted. The altitude decision was Griffin's most important of the battle, and it turned out to be disastrous.

At 0830hrs, *Hornet*'s outgoing strike warned of Japanese aircraft inbound. Both carriers prepared to launch all ready aircraft to empty the flight decks before the arrival of the Japanese. Task-Force 16's CAP was reinforced to 22 fighters, half at 10,000ft and the other half headed up to that altitude. *Hornet* added another seven, for a total of 15; a total of 37 fighters were airborne.

As the Japanese strike continued inbound, neither the radar on *Enterprise* nor on *Hornet* detected anything. The CXAM radar on cruiser *Northampton* did detect the incoming strike at 0841hrs to the northwest at 70 miles and the information was passed by flag signal to *Hornet*, but reached its FDO late and never reached Griffin on *Enterprise*.

At 0853hrs, Murata's carrier attack plane squadron from *Shokaku* spotted ships which were soon confirmed as a carrier, two cruisers, and four destroyers. This was *Hornet* and TF-17; clouds covered TF-16. Murata ordered an immediate attack. He had two groups: at 17,000ft were 21 carrier bombers from *Zuikaku* with eight escorting Zeros at 21,000ft in a trail position; the second group consisted of 20 *Shokaku* torpedo-armed carrier attack planes at 14,000ft with an escort of four Zeros.

TF-17 maneuvering to avoid air attack. *Hornet* is visible to the left. This shot was taken by one of *Hornet*'s returning aircraft. (Naval History and Heritage Command)

▼ EVENTS

1 0830hrs – *Hornet*'s outgoing strike warns of Japanese aircraft inbound. *Hornet* adds another seven Wildcats on CAP to augment the eight already at 10,000ft.

2 0853hrs – Strike commander Lt. Cdr. Murata Shigeharu spots TF-17 and orders an immediate attack. He has two groups: 21 carrier bombers from *Zuikaku* with eight escorting Zeros and 20 *Shokaku* torpedo-armed carrier attack planes with an escort of four Zeros.

3 0855hrs – *Hornet*'s radar finally detects Japanese aircraft 35 miles to the west-southwest. TF-16 moves eight fighters to the west to assist TF-17.

4 0859hrs – *Hornet*'s fighters spot the Japanese, but cannot react in time. Murata deploys his torpedo aircraft in two groups to attack in an anvil formation from both bows of *Hornet*. He leads 11 torpedo planes with the four fighters to the south diving to gain speed; the remaining nine torpedo planes head in from the north.

5 0858hrs – Dive-bombers under Lt. Takahashi Sadamu spot TF-17 and attack first. His squadron is deployed in three groups of seven aircraft with eight escort Zeros above and to the rear. Eight *Hornet* Wildcats gain enough altitude to conduct a head-on attack and destroy three dive-bombers and severely damage three others. The Zeros shoot down three Wildcats. The *Hornet* fighters at lower altitudes are able only to down a single dive-bomber.

6 0910hrs – The first group of carrier bombers begin their dives astern of *Hornet*. Of the seven carrier bombers, three score hits on the carrier and four survive.

7 0915hrs – The first group of torpedo planes attack led by Murata. The escorting Zeros intervene against intercepting Wildcats and shoot down two for the loss of a single Zero. Murata's plan of executing an anvil attack from ahead of *Hornet* is thwarted when the carrier changes course to the northeast. This forces Murata's group to conduct a tactically disadvantageous stern attack. The first section to attack is Murata's which approaches *Hornet* from her starboard quarter.

It does not launch from a good angle, but the attack is devastating. The first torpedo strikes *Hornet* amidships and, within seconds, the next torpedo strikes aft in the engineering spaces. The next section of three torpedo bombers misses with its torpedoes to starboard. The attack angle for the final five aircraft is even worse. Three attack *Hornet* and miss, and the final two attack heavy cruiser *Pensacola* with no success. The Japanese lose five aircraft.

8 0914hrs – The second group of *Zuikaku* carrier bombers moving to the north run into TF-16 fighters coming south to assist *Hornet*. Of the six carrier bombers, one is destroyed. Five attack *Hornet* just as Murata's torpedo planes are attacking. Four attack *Hornet*, but all miss. The last aircraft crashes on the carrier.

9 0914hrs – Final group of carrier bombers is intercepted by *Enterprise* fighters. Three survive to attack *Hornet*, but all miss. Only one survives subsequent Wildcat attacks while leaving the area of TF-17.

10 0914hrs – Nine *Shokaku* carrier attack planes coming in from the north without escort are attacked by Wildcats. Three are shot down; one attempts to crash light cruiser *Juneau*, but is shot down in the attempt. Five approach the screen and one is shot down by destroyer *Morris*. The remaining four close to within 300–800 yards of *Hornet* before releasing their torpedoes, but all miss.

11 0917hrs – A single carrier bomber drops its bomb 50 yards off *Hornet*'s bow, then returns to crash into the ship forward on the port side. One minute later, a carrier attack plane from the second group which had previously jettisoned its torpedo attempts to crash onto *Hornet*, but hits the water forward of the ship.

12 0925hrs – Last air combat between the CAP and the retreating Japanese. *Hornet* is crippled and is dead in the water from two torpedo hits, three bomb hits, and two crashed aircraft. The Japanese lose a total of five fighters, 17 carrier bombers, and 16 carrier attack planes. Six Wildcats are lost.

ATTACK ON *HORNET*
The Japanese assault destroys the US carrier.

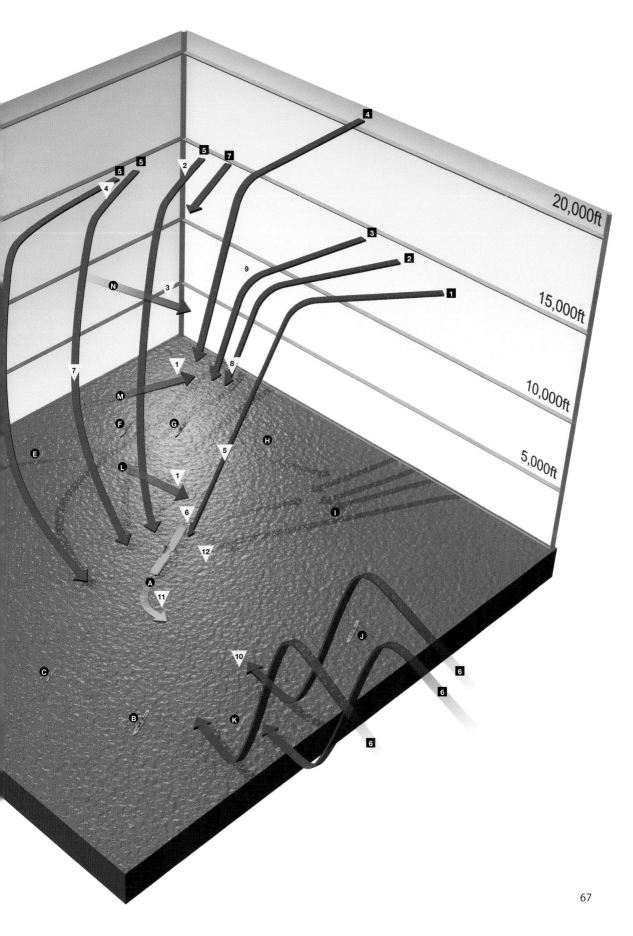

20,000ft

15,000ft

10,000ft

5,000ft

67

At 0855hrs, *Hornet*'s radar finally detected a group of bogeys 35 miles to the west-southwest. *Enterprise* also picked up the same contact at 45 miles. Griffin moved eight fighters to the west, and the pilots decided to climb above 10,000ft. At 0859hrs, *Hornet*'s fighters spotted the Japanese, but it was already too late. Murata deployed his torpedo aircraft in two groups to attack in an anvil formation from both bows of the carrier. He led 11 torpedo planes with the four fighters to the south diving to gain speed; the remaining nine torpedo planes came in from the north. The dive-bombers spotted *Hornet* at 0858hrs. The Japanese had achieved a fully coordinated attack.

The dive-bombers under Lt. Takahashi Sadamu attacked first. His squadron was deployed on three groups of seven aircraft with the eight Zeros above them and to the rear. Eight *Hornet* Wildcats had gained enough altitude to conduct a head-on attack on the approaching carrier bombers and the Japanese formation was shattered by the attack with only a single seven-aircraft group not suffering heavily. The Zeros flying cover managed to shoot down three Wildcats and chase the others off, but not before the American fighters had shot down at least three dive-bombers and severely damaged three others. The second group of *Hornet* fighters was able only to shoot down a single dive-bomber. By 0910hrs, the Japanese were beginning their attack runs on *Hornet*. Griffin sent his part of TF-16's CAP south to help defend *Hornet*.

As the Japanese prepared to attack, TF-17 increased speed to 28 knots and, at 0903hrs, changed course to the northeast. *Hornet* was positioned with a ring of escorts deployed in a circle 2,000 yards from the carrier. At 0905hrs, *Hornet* spotted the first Japanese aircraft, seven dive-bombers, coming in from the west. Minutes later, the ship's 5in. guns opened fire at 10,500 yards. The effectiveness of the antiaircraft fire was much reduced by the beautifully executed attack which split up the antiaircraft defenses.

The first group of carrier bombers began their dives at 0910hrs, emerging at 5,000ft astern of *Hornet* through a cloud. The first aircraft dropped its bomb but missed to starboard. The second placed a 550-pound semi-armor-piercing bomb in the center of the flight deck abeam the island which penetrated three decks. The third carrier bomber was destroyed by antiaircraft fire before it could release its bomb and landed in the water 30ft from *Hornet*'s starboard

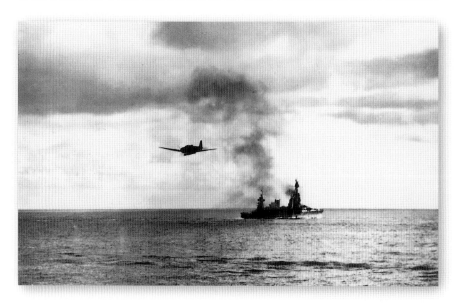

One of Murata's Type 97 carrier attack planes during its attack run against *Hornet*. The aircraft has yet to drop its torpedo. The photo was taken from heavy cruiser *Pensacola* with heavy cruiser *Northampton* in the background. (Naval History and Heritage Command)

bow. The next aircraft made a successful attack with a high-explosive bomb which hit the flight deck aft, only 20ft from the starboard edge. The blast created an 11ft hole in the flight deck and caused heavy casualties to nearby gun crews. The aircraft was hit by 20mm gunfire and crashed but not before the rear crewmen bailed out by parachute. He lived and remarkably was picked up by a Japanese destroyer the next day. The fifth carrier bomber circled ahead to approach *Hornet* from her port bow. This aircraft also scored a hit with a semi-armor-piercing bomb which struck near the second hit and passed through four decks causing a heavy loss of life. The next aircraft also circled around to attack from the bow, but missed. The seventh and final aircraft was already crippled by Wildcats and never reached *Hornet*. Its bomb hit in the carrier's wake soon followed by the aircraft itself. By any measure, the results of the first dive-bombing attack were impressive. Of the seven carrier bombers to attack, three scored hits and four survived.

Now the torpedo planes commenced their attack. Their escort intervened against intercepting Wildcats, shooting down two for the loss of a single Zero. Murata's plan of executing an anvil attack from ahead of *Hornet* was upset when TF-17 changed course to the northeast. This forced Murata's group into a tactically disadvantageous stern attack. The 11 torpedo planes increased speed to at least get a beam shot while *Hornet*'s captain attempted to keep his stern to the attackers to give them as small a target as possible. The first group to attack consisted of the three planes led by Murata. Flying at 300ft, they approached *Hornet* from her starboard quarter. The first Type 97 carrier attack plane dropped its torpedo from 1,500 yards and then was shot down. The next two closed to within 1,000 yards before dropping their weapons. After banking away, Murata's aircraft was hit and crashed off *Hornet*'s starboard side. The third aircraft survived.

Though they did not launch from a good angle, the attack was devastating. At 0915hrs, the first torpedo struck *Hornet* amidships just aft of the island. Within seconds, the next torpedo struck aft in the engineering spaces. The third torpedo just missed ahead. The results were immediate. The forward engine room and two firerooms were knocked out by flooding, causing the ship to lose power and come to a stop and the ship took a 10-degree starboard list. The next group of three torpedo bombers followed a minute later. The first

aircraft was shot down after jettisoning its torpedo, and the other two missed with their torpedoes to starboard. As *Hornet* continued its turn to the northwest, the attack angle for the final five aircraft became even worse. The next group of three passed through the screen to attack *Hornet*. One aircraft jettisoned its torpedo and was shot down exiting the formation; the other two missed with their torpedoes but survived. The final two aircraft decided to attack heavy cruiser *Pensacola*. One launched its torpedo and missed, and the other, after catching fire from antiaircraft fire, attempted to crash into the cruiser. It missed *Pensacola*'s bow by only a few feet before hitting the water. Murata's torpedo bombers had delivered the most important blows of the entire battle. From his 11 aircraft, eight torpedoes were launched at *Hornet* and two struck. Five carrier attack planes were shot down.

The second group of *Zuikaku* carrier bombers moved to the north to attack *Hornet* where they ran into the *Enterprise* fighters coming south to assist *Hornet*. Of the six carrier bombers, one aircraft was destroyed before it entered a dive while the other five attacked just as Murata's torpedo bombers were doing their deadly work. The remaining dive-bombers attacked from 12,000ft from *Hornet*'s port side. Four attacked *Hornet*, but none scored a hit. The last carrier bomber was already in flames when it appeared over *Hornet* at 0914hrs. The pilot (if still alive) decided to crash his aircraft onto the carrier and the plane's starboard wing hit the edge of the ship's stack while the fuselage bounced off the island and penetrated the flight deck. The resulting fires burned for two hours.

The final group of carrier bombers was the least successful. Three aircraft were lost in the initial Wildcat interception, and the remaining aircraft turned south. At 0914hrs, they were intercepted by *Enterprise* fighters at 13,000ft. One dive-bomber was shot down in its dive, but three more pressed the attack. All missed *Hornet*, but only one survived subsequent Wildcat attacks while leaving the area of TF-17.

The last group to attack consisted of the nine *Shokaku* carrier attack planes coming in from the north. These had no Zero escort and were assailed by Wildcats. Three were shot down, and one attempted to crash into the

The battle of Santa Cruz, October 26, 1942, 1200–2400hrs

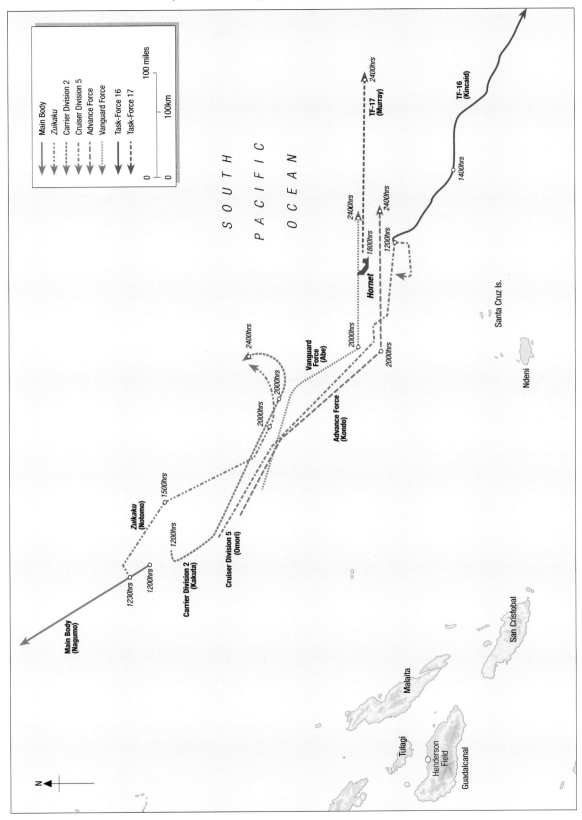

Legend:
- Main Body
- *Zuikaku*
- Carrier Division 2
- Cruiser Division 5
- Advance Force
- Vanguard Force
- Task-Force 16
- Task-Force 17

100 miles
100km

SOUTH PACIFIC OCEAN

TF-17 (Murray) — 2400hrs
TF-16 (Kincaid) — 1400hrs
1200hrs
2400hrs
2400hrs
Hornet — 1800hrs
2000hrs
2000hrs
2000hrs

Vanguard Force (Abe)
Advance Force (Kondo)

2400hrs
2000hrs
2000hrs

Santa Cruz Is.
Ndeni

1500hrs
1200hrs

Zuikaku (Notomo)

Carrier Division 2 (Kakuta)

Cruiser Division 5 (Omori)

1200hrs
1230hrs

Main Body (Nagumo)

San Cristobal
Malaita
Tulagi
Henderson Field
Guadalcanal

N

Hornet seen during the attack from *Shokaku*'s torpedo planes and *Zuikaku*'s dive-bombers. The carrier is already listing to starboard because of two torpedo hits and a fire is burning aft as a result of one of the bomb hits. (Naval History and Heritage Command)

light cruiser *Juneau*, but was shot down in the attempt. The remaining five approached the screen, and another was shot down by destroyer *Morris*. The surviving four closed to within 300–800 yards of *Hornet*'s bows before releasing their torpedoes, but scored no hits.

The last attacks on *Hornet* were from two aircraft crippled by the Wildcats. The first appeared at 0917hrs off the carrier's stern. Already smoking, the carrier bomber attempted to drop its bomb from a shallow dive, but it landed off the bow by some 50 yards. Then the Japanese pilot pulled up off his dive, reversed course over *Northampton*, and headed back to *Hornet* with the obvious intent of crashing onto the ship. The pilot skillfully passed ahead of the bow and then crashed into the ship forward on the port side. The body of the plane penetrated through the gallery deck and landed in the forward elevator pit starting a fire. Only a minute later, a carrier attack plane from the northern group which had previously jettisoned its torpedo returned to crash into the carrier. It approached *Hornet* from dead ahead, but the wounded aircraft crashed in the water before reaching the ship.

As the last air combat took place between the American CAP and the retreating Japanese, it was possible to take account. The attack represented the finest, and certainly the last, coordinated strike by Japanese aircraft on an American carrier. The result was serious damage to *Hornet* – she was left dead in the water from two torpedoes, three bomb hits, and two crashed aircraft. *Hornet* was without power to fight fires or conduct flight operations, though counter-flooding reduced the list to only two degrees. The price paid for this success was very high. The Japanese delivered 53 attack aircraft over TF-17. Of these, only a fraction was recovered safely. Of the 12 fighters,

Japanese losses in the attack on TF-17, by cause			
	Zero fighters	Carrier bombers	Carrier attack planes
Starting	12	21	20
Lost to CAP	3	7	2
Lost to AA fire	0	4	8
Ditched on return	2	6	6
Survived	7	4	4

seven returned; of 21 carrier bombers, a mere four returned; and of the 20 carrier attack planes, again only four returned. In exchange, the Americans lost six Wildcats, though two pilots were later rescued.

The second Japanese wave had an opportunity to convert a promising beginning to the battle into a decisive victory. By 0945hrs, *Enterprise*'s CAP numbered only 11 fighters. Kinkaid turned TF-16 to the southeast at 27 knots and headed into some rain squalls. By 1000hrs, the CAP was down to only eight fighters and a strike of ten unescorted Dauntlesses from VB-10 was being refueled and re-armed on the carrier's deck.

Enterprise's movements were already known to the Japanese. Japanese monitoring of American radio circuits, in particular the FDO circuit which kept referring to REAPER (*Enterprise*) and BLUE (*Hornet*) Bases, confirmed there were at least two carriers active. This was confirmed by the 0920hrs sighting report of *Enterprise* from the first attack wave and updated when the tracking plane from *Zuikaku* radioed a 0937hrs report of *Enterprise*'s location.

Unlike the first wave, the second Japanese wave approached in two groups. The first consisted of 19 carrier bombers from *Shokaku* escorted by five Zeros. These approached *Enterprise* at 16,140ft. Forty-five minutes behind these were 17 carrier attack planes with torpedoes from *Zuikaku* escorted by four Zeros. The first American detection of the incoming second wave was by heavy cruiser *Northampton*'s radar at about 0930hrs when the *Shokaku* dive-bombers were detected to the northwest at 76 miles. At about 0945hrs, the first ship in TF-16 gained contact at 55 miles when *South Dakota* raised the alarm. Again, the radar on *Enterprise* proved deficient and did not gain contact on the large group of bogeys until they were only 45 miles out.

The leader of the *Shokaku* carrier bombers, Lieutenant-Commander Seki Mamoru spotted *Hornet* first but quickly discerned she was heavily damaged. He led his group to the east and soon spotted TF-16 20 miles beyond. At 1008hrs, he ordered his group to attack. As the Japanese aircraft approached, Kinkaid brought TF-16 into a starboard turn and headed to the southwest. *Enterprise*'s CAP was not well positioned. Eight fighters were overhead at 10,000ft while another 13 circled at lower altitudes. Potentially most damaging, the strike of ten Dauntlesses was still in various stages of being fueled and armed on the carrier's flight and hangar decks.

After the initial Japanese attack, *Hornet* was left dead in the water and listing to starboard. A destroyer is alongside and *Northampton* is standing by. (Naval History and Heritage Command)

JUNYO ATTACKS (pp. 74–75)

Following the attack of Carrier Division 1, _Junyo_'s strike of 17 carrier bombers approached TF-16. At 1120hrs, the leader of the strike spotted _Enterprise_ and ordered an immediate attack. The dive-bombers were not intercepted by _Enterprise_'s CAP, but encountered clouds over the carrier which prevented the formation from gaining good dive positions and prevented all the attackers from tracking _Enterprise_. A group of eight dive-bombers **(1)** dove on _Enterprise_ **(2)** from astern but their shallow 45-degree dives made them vulnerable to antiaircraft fire **(3)**. Each of the Type 99 Carrier Bombers was engaged in sequence as it attacked _Enterprise_. Four of the dive-bombers were shot down in exchange for a single near miss **(4)** on the carrier.

The initial orders from the FDO were ineffective. Griffin sent most of the fighters to the northeast to intercept, but since he had no information on the altitude of the Japanese, he did not order the Wildcats to climb. Seki formed his 19 carrier bombers into three groups which he deployed in line astern to attack out of the sun. They headed toward TF-16 almost from due north and approached *Enterprise* from her starboard side. Because the American fighters were at a lower altitude, Seki's dive-bombers reached their pushover point largely unmolested. Only two American fighters engaged the Japanese aircraft before they began their dive, and only a single Japanese aircraft was shot down at 1014hrs. Though the American CAP was ineffective in defending TF-16, the antiaircraft fire of the American ships proved deadly. When the attack began at 1015hrs, the heavy antiaircraft batteries on *Enterprise* and *South Dakota*, trailing the carrier by 2,500 yards, engaged each dive-bomber in succession as it conducted its attack.

Seki and three other carrier bombers were shot down, and none of the aircraft scored a hit on *Enterprise*. Two minutes later, the next group of seven aircraft attacked the carrier from astern. The lead bomber in this group dove through the heavy antiaircraft fire to place a 550-pound high-explosive bomb in the middle of the flight deck only 20ft from the bow at 1017hrs. Damage was light since it went through the flight deck, through the forecastle and then exploded in air off the port bow. One Dauntless on the bow was blown over the side and another pushed over deliberately to put out a small fire. A minute later, a second hit, this one with a semi-armor-piercing bomb, landed 10ft abaft of the forward elevator in the center of the flight deck. An explosion in the hangar deck created a fire that resulted in six Dauntlesses being tossed over the side to avoid feeding it. The bomb continued to the second deck where a repair party was killed and a fire started in the well of the forward elevator. Another near miss very close aboard the starboard quarter was recorded at 1020hrs. This opened underwater seams and resulted in another Wildcat being blown overboard and a Dauntless being pushed overboard. The aircraft which scored the near miss was engaged by fighters on the way out and destroyed.

Of the 12 carrier bombers from the second and third groups, only one bombed accurately enough to gain a damaging near miss. Losses were extremely high with six aircraft shot down, including two destroyed by fighters before they could attack, another by fighters after it had dropped its bomb, and another three by antiaircraft fire. Overall, the Japanese lost ten of 19 carrier bombers with three destroyed by fighters and seven from antiaircraft fire.

LEFT
The height of the dive-bombing attack from *Shokaku's* aircraft against *Enterprise*. This photo shows the intensity of the antiaircraft fire. *Enterprise* is at left and *South Dakota* is at right. At least two of the Type 99 carrier bombers are visible over *Enterprise*. (Naval History and Heritage Command)

RIGHT
At 1020hrs, one of the last of *Shokaku's* Type 99 carrier bombers placed its weapon only 10ft off *Enterprise's* starboard quarter. In addition to opening submerged hull plates, a VB-10 Dauntless ended up precariously balanced on the starboard 20mm gallery. Deck crews tried to push the aircraft over the side which was finally accomplished when Captain Hardison aided their efforts by putting the carrier into a hard port turn. (Naval History and Heritage Command)

JAPANESE FORCES
1 *Shokaku* Carrier Bomber Squadron (7 Type 99 carrier bombers)
2 *Shokaku* Carrier Bomber Squadron (7 Type 99 carrier bombers)
3 *Shokaku* Carrier Bomber Squadron (5 Type 99 carrier bombers)
4 *Shokaku* Fighter Unit (5 A6M Type 0 fighters)
5 *Zuikaku* Carrier Attack Squadron (8 Type 97 carrier attack planes)
6 *Zuikaku* Carrier Attack Squadron (8 Type 97 carrier attack planes)
7 *Zuikaku* Carrier Fighter Squadron (4 A6M Type 0 fighters

AMERICAN FORCES
A *Enterprise*
B *South Dakota*
C *Smith*
D *Mahan*
E *Portland*
F *Cushing*
G *Maury*
H *San Juan*
I *Preston*
J *Conygham*
K VF-10 CAP at 10,000ft (8 F4F)
L VF-10 CAP at lower altitudes (13 F4F)

EVENTS

1 1008hrs – Lieutenant-Commander Seki Mamoru orders his Carrier Bomber Squadron to attack *Enterprise*. He divides his 19 carrier bombers into three groups and approaches *Enterprise* from the north.

2 1014hrs – Seki's seven dive-bombers reach their pushover point unmolested by Wildcats.

3 1015hrs – Dive-bombing attack begins from *Enterprise*'s starboard quarter. Four aircraft are shot down by antiaircraft fire and no hits are scored.

4 1017hrs – Next group of seven aircraft attack from astern. The lead bomber hits *Enterprise* in the forward section of the flight deck but damage is light. At 1018hrs a second bomb hit causes an explosion in the hangar deck creating a fire.

5 1020hrs – Third group of dive-bombers gains a near miss very close aboard the starboard quarter which opens underwater seams.

6 1035hrs – Radar aboard *Enterprise* detects a large group of aircraft to the northwest. CAP is now 11 Wildcats at altitude and an additional 14 at low altitude.

7 1038hrs – Leader of *Zuikaku* Carrier Attack Squadron,

Lieutenant Imajuku Shigeichiro, makes visual contact with TF-16 and orders an attack. He divides his force into two 8-plane groups to attack *Enterprise* from each bow. The first group heads south through a bank of clouds while the second group continues to the southeast with all four escorting Zeros.

8 1046hrs – Imajuku's aircraft is shot down by Wildcats, but the remainder of his group is not attacked by CAP. The first torpedo is launched from *Enterprise*'s starboard beam and misses. *Enterprise* makes a sharp turn to starboard and evades the next three. The last aircraft of the first group attacks *Enterprise* from dead ahead and misses. Five of the eight aircraft are shot down.

9 1048hrs – Two aircraft from the first group attack *South Dakota* with no success.

10 1047hrs – Second group commences attack. Wildcats destroy one and force another to abort. One crippled aircraft crashes into destroyer *Smith*.

11 1052hrs – Five aircraft drop on *Enterprise* from astern and all miss. Three aircraft from the second group are shot down. All told, nine Type 97 carrier attack planes attack *Enterprise*, but all torpedoes miss.

THE JAPANESE CARRIER AIRCRAFT ATTACK ON THE AMERICAN CARRIER *ENTERPRISE*

Aircraft from the *Zuikaku* and *Shokaku* attempt to disable the US fleet carrier.

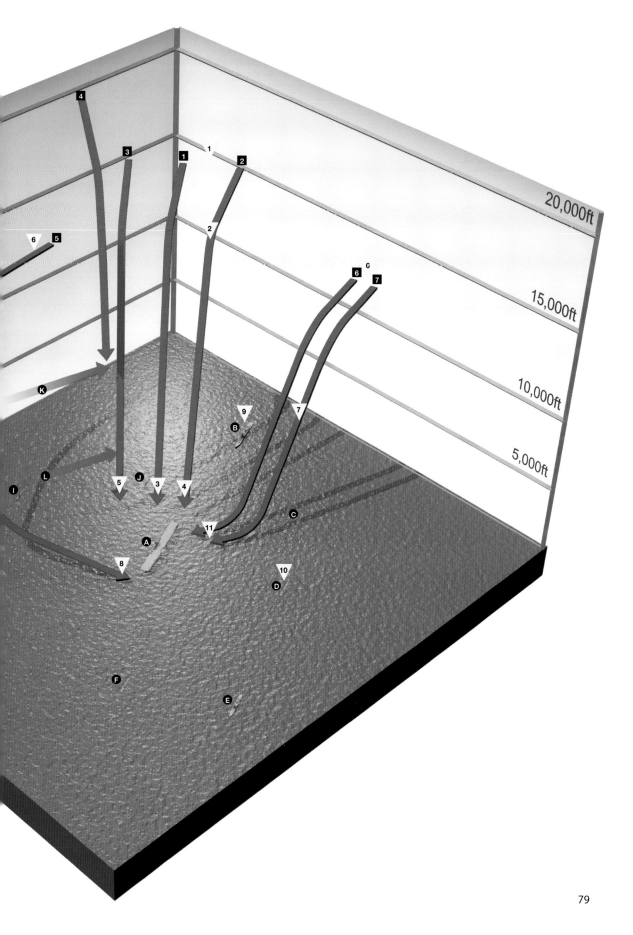

20,000ft

15,000ft

10,000ft

5,000ft

79

A *Zuikaku* Type 97 carrier attack plane after dropping its torpedo against *Enterprise* heads toward battleship *South Dakota* to exit the formation of TF-16. This remarkable view was taken from the port side of *Enterprise*'s island. (Naval History and Heritage Command)

Damage to *Enterprise* was not serious. However, 44 crewmen were dead and ten aircraft (one fighter and nine Dauntlesses) destroyed. The Japanese claimed six hits and radioed at 1030hrs that the carrier was burning and listing to starboard.

At the conclusion of the dive-bomber attacks, Griffin instructed 11 Wildcats to gain altitude in expectation of a follow-up attack. An additional 14 fighters were circling at low altitude. The first indication of another attack was gained at 1035hrs when the radar aboard *Enterprise* detected a large group of bogies to the northwest. Griffin was able to position his CAP better for this round. He warned his airborne fighters at 1044hrs that the enemy was to the northwest at 15 miles and was composed of torpedo bombers.

This was the carrier attack plane squadron from *Zuikaku* approaching TF-16 at about 13,000ft. At 1035hrs, the flight leader, Lieutenant Imajuku Shigeichiro made visual contact with TF-17. Minutes later, he saw the TF-16 steaming to the southwest. He chose the seemingly undamaged carrier for attack. His plan was to divide his force into two eight-plane groups to attack the carrier from each bow. The first group headed south through a bank of clouds while the second group with all four fighters continued heading to the southeast through the same bank of clouds.

Imajuku's eight aircraft attacked first. Since they were unescorted, Imajuku moved to wave-top level some distance from TF-16. Only a single aircraft was engaged by fighters before reaching TF-16; this was Imajuku's aircraft shot down at about 1046hrs. His wingman launched his torpedo from *Enterprise*'s starboard beam and missed. The next section came in from *Enterprise*'s starboard bow and launched its torpedoes. *Enterprise* made a sharp turn to starboard and was successful in evading all three. The final section of two aircraft was unable to get a proper attack position on *Enterprise* so went after *South Dakota* trailing astern. The first aircraft released its torpedo and missed, but the second aircraft was set afire by antiaircraft fire and continued to approach the massive battleship. The pilot got close enough actually to launch its torpedo over *South Dakota*'s stern so that it entered the water 20 yards off her port quarter. The aircraft crashed 200 yards farther away.

The last aircraft from Imajuku's section conducted his attack run from dead ahead of *Enterprise*. The torpedo was not sighted until it was 800 yards away, and a sharp turn made it miss only 100 yards off the starboard side. The aircraft was shot down by the quadruple 1.1in. antiaircraft gun mounted on the carrier's bow.

The second group of eight aircraft was roughly handled as it dropped through the clouds. Two Wildcats caught the Japanese aircraft in their descent and were able to destroy one, heavily damage another, make another abort, and damage several others. The Zero escorts were unable to intervene. When the six remaining aircraft (including the heavily damaged one) emerged from the clouds, they were astern of TF-16. While moving through the escort screen, one carrier attack plane which had been set afire either by a pursuing Wildcat or by antiaircraft fire decided it could not attack the carrier and instead chose to dive on the destroyer *Smith*. The aircraft struck the destroyer at 1047hrs on 5in. mount number two, just forward of the bridge. The entire forward section of the destroyer was soon in flames from the fuel aboard the aircraft and then from the aircraft's torpedo exploding.

The remaining five torpedo planes attempted to get a launch position off the carrier's port bow. The carrier attempted to keep its stern to the approaching Japanese in order to present as small a target as possible. One of the five launched its torpedo from dead astern and was shot down by antiaircraft fire. The torpedo missed. The last four launched torpedoes from the carrier's port quarter, but only one even came close. The attack was over at 1052hrs. Wildcats shot down two more carrier attack planes on their way out of the battle area.

The torpedo plane attack against *Enterprise* was the key point in the battle. If even a single torpedo had hit *Enterprise*, it could have meant disaster. In the three previous carrier battles, any time that a Japanese air-launched torpedo hit a carrier, it was enough to start a chain of events leading to the loss of the ship. The same fate awaited *Hornet* at Santa Cruz. Of the 16 torpedo planes which began the attack, nine launched their

Destroyer *Smith* on fire after being crashed into by a *Shokaku* Type 97 carrier attack plane. This view is from *South Dakota*. (Naval History and Heritage Command)

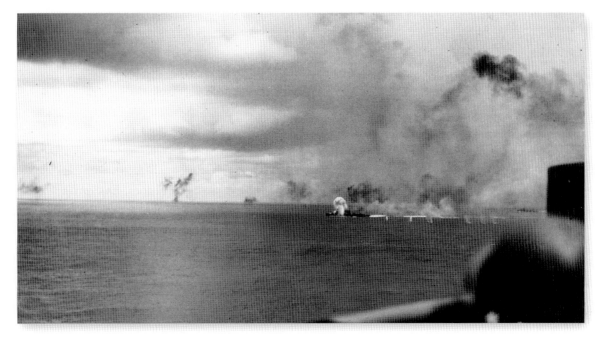

THE END OF *HORNET* (pp. 82–83)

The Advance Force observed flashes from the gunfire of destroyers *Mustin* and *Anderson* at 2035hrs as the American ships carried out their orders to scuttle *Hornet*. Kondo ordered several destroyers to pursue and destroy the American ships. At 2214hrs lead elements of the Advance Force arrived in the vicinity of *Hornet*. The carrier was listing 45 degrees to port and was consumed by flame **(1)**. After Kondo broke off the pursuit of the Americans, destroyers *Akigumo* and *Makigumo* returned to *Hornet* at 2200hrs to determine if the ship could be salvaged. The Japanese investigated the wreck and determined salvage was impossible and determined *Hornet*'s identity from the small "8" hull numbers (she carried no number on her flight deck). *Akigumo* and *Makigumo* **(2)** each fired two torpedoes **(3)** to finish off the carrier. All four were seen to hit, and the carrier finally sank at 0135hrs.

weapons at *Enterprise*. On this occasion, the CAP had done a credible job by savaging one of the two groups of torpedo planes and disrupting the coordination between the two groups. A single Wildcat pilot was credited with five torpedo planes shot down. The escape of *Enterprise* was certainly a close-run thing.

In a bizarre set of events, TF-16 suffered another loss just before the arrival of Seki's dive-bombers. Two *Enterprise* Avengers returned just before 1000hrs. One still had its torpedo aboard. Since the *Enterprise* could not land them at that time, the pilot of the damaged Avenger ditched his aircraft near destroyer *Porter*. Soon after the aircraft entered the water, one of *Porter*'s lookouts spotted a torpedo to port. It was the Mark XIII torpedo from the ditched Avenger now running in circles. At 1004hrs, it struck *Porter* amidships in her engineering spaces, bringing the ship to a halt. The unfortunate destroyer was scuttled by Kinkaid's command just after noon.

The last Japanese carrier was also preparing to strike. The Advance Force was moving to close the range to the American carriers. Kakuta planned for his strike to be launched at 0905hrs from an estimated 280 miles from TF-61. The first wave consisted of 12 Zeros and 17 carrier bombers, followed by a second strike of seven carrier attack planes. After the launch of this strike, Kondo detached *Junyo* and two destroyers to operate with Nagumo and took the rest of the Advance Force to the southeast in search of the American task forces.

As *Junyo*'s strike approached TF-16, the radar on *Enterprise* ceased working. While the incoming strike was detected by the SC radar aboard *South Dakota* to the west at 45 miles, this information never got to the FDO. When *Enterprise*'s radar came back on line at 1115hrs, it detected a large group of unknown aircraft at 20 miles. The airborne CAP had no time to react to this information and was not helped by Griffin's vague directions. At 1121hrs, the first of *Junyo*'s dive-bombers appeared out of the clouds above *Enterprise*. The leader of the *Junyo* dive-bombers had sighted *Hornet* dead in the water at 1040hrs, but continued on in search of more important prey after officers on *Junyo* countermanded his intention to attack *Hornet*'s cruiser escort. At 1120hrs, he spotted TF-16 through a break in the clouds and ordered an immediate attack. They were not intercepted by fighters, but the clouds prevented them from getting the best attack position. Consequently, the dive-bombers dove on *Enterprise* from astern but in a shallow 45-degree dive which made them vulnerable to antiaircraft fire. A group of eight carrier bombers was the first to attack. The first three all missed and all were destroyed by antiaircraft fire. The lead aircraft in the next section of three aircraft dropped his bomb less than 10ft off the port

LEFT
One of *Junyo*'s dive bombers places a bomb near *Enterprise*'s starboard side during the 1100hrs attack. None of the eight *Junyo* dive-bombers which attacked *Enterprise* gained a direct hit. (Naval History and Heritage Command)

RIGHT
Heavy cruiser *Northampton* was assigned the mission of towing *Hornet* out of the battle area. The attempt was ultimately unsuccessful since there was no air cover to prevent additional attacks on the crippled carrier. After a third torpedo hit on *Hornet*, the effort was abandoned. (Naval History and Heritage Command)

bow which opened plating to the sea and knocked out the mechanism controlling the jammed forward elevator. The next four aircraft all missed.

The other group of nine dive-bombers lost contact with *Enterprise* in the low clouds. As a result, they ended up conducting disjointed attacks against the now spread-out TF-16 beginning at 1129hrs. Four broke out of the clouds above *South Dakota* and dove on the battleship. The first three bombs missed, but the last hit the heavily armored top of the forward 16in. turret. The turret was undamaged, but the shrapnel wounded several, including the ship's captain. The remaining five carrier bombers attacked the antiaircraft cruiser *San Juan* off *Enterprise*'s port bow. The first three bombers missed at 1132hrs, while the fourth scored a damaging near miss on the port side. The last aircraft placed an armor-piercing bomb on the cruiser's stern which passed all the way through the thinly armored ship before exploding under the hull. This resulted in flooding in several compartments and temporarily jammed the rudder. None of the nine aircraft was hit by antiaircraft fire, but four were destroyed by fighters and Dauntlesses while exiting the battle area. Of the five carrier bombers surviving from the first group, American aircraft accounted for another carrier bomber destroyed and another heavily damaged. The 12 escorting *Junyo* fighters suffered no losses, and probably accounted for two Wildcats and an Avenger.

The full exchange of carrier strikes from TF-61 and the four Japanese carriers had resulted in heavy damage to both sides. Two of the four Japanese carriers were out of action. *Hornet* remained dead in the water and *Enterprise* was damaged, but still in action. Nevertheless, the Japanese had gained the upper hand and sought to finish off the surviving American flight deck.

Nagumo and his staff tried to make sense of the morning's action and decided that three American carriers were in action. One was the cripple often sighted during the morning and the other two were operating to the north and northwest of the cripple. At 1132hrs, Nagumo radioed this assessment. Since the actual position of *Enterprise* was now south of *Hornet*, this erroneous assessment had the effect of leading later Japanese attacks off *Enterprise*'s trail.

Nagumo's means to conduct additional attacks were limited by the heavy losses from the morning attacks. The surviving aircraft from the first wave started to recover on *Zuikaku* at 1140hrs and some were directed to *Junyo* located to the southwest. The recovery was completed by 1230hrs, but the total haul was only ten fighters, eight carrier attack planes and one carrier bomber aboard *Zuikaku* and two fighters, four carrier bombers and one carrier attack plane on *Junyo*. Thirteen aircraft from the first wave were forced to ditch – two fighters, six carrier bombers and five carrier attack planes. During the recovery, *Junyo* steamed close to *Zuikaku* and Nagumo detached his last surviving carrier and five destroyers to operate with *Junyo*. Nagumo and his staff were stuck onboard his flagship *Shokaku* now heading out of the combat area at 31 knots. Meanwhile, Kondo had ordered the Vanguard Force to break off its northwesterly heading and steam toward the Support Force which was heading toward the last known position of the Americans.

As the Japanese prepared to mount additional strikes, Kinkaid faced a very different situation. *Hornet* was dead in the water and attempts by heavy cruiser *Northampton* to begin towing the carrier were only partially unsuccessful. *Enterprise* was damaged, and Kinkaid faced the prospect of landing all aloft aircraft on a single deck with no functioning forward elevator. He was certain that one or two undamaged Japanese carriers remained, and was unable to provide CAP over the crippled *Hornet*. To remain in the battle only risked losing *Enterprise*, which would have been calamitous. With all this in mind, Kinkaid made the correct decision to withdraw. At 1135hrs, he informed Halsey of his decision.

It was critical that *Enterprise* recovered the aircraft from the two strikes and from CAP duty. As many as 73 aircraft were aloft – 28 Wildcats, 24 Dauntlesses and 21 Avengers. In the first phase of the recovery, 23 Wildcats and all 24 Dauntlesses were brought on board until the deck was unable to handle any more. Five fighters were forced to ditch. At 1235hrs, with the Avengers still aloft and while *Enterprise* respotted the deck and moved aircraft into the hangar bay, TF-16 changed course to the southeast and increased speed to 27 knots to exit the area. As soon as aircraft could be fueled and re-armed, 25 Wildcats were sent back into the air beginning at 1251hrs. Finally, ten of the Avengers were recovered and another decided to go to Espiritu Santo. Afterwards 13 Dauntlesses were sent to Espiritu Santo to ease the congestion. *Enterprise* still had 84 aircraft onboard (41 fighters, 33 dive-bombers, and ten Avengers). The disaster of losing the bulk of the aircraft from two air groups had been averted.

At 1300hrs, Yamamoto issued orders to Kondo to pursue and destroy the retreating Americans. This would be accomplished in one of two ways. The Japanese still retained two operating flight decks. Admiral Kakuta on *Junyo* and Captain Nomoto on *Zuikaku* both prepared to launch follow-up strikes with their remaining aircraft. Meanwhile, both Kondo's Advance Force and the heavy units from the Vanguard Force were attempting to close on the Americans.

The first follow-up strike from *Junyo* was sent off at 1313hrs to fly to the southeast out to a distance of 260 miles. It consisted of eight Zeros (from three different parent carriers) and seven carrier attack planes (only six carried torpedoes). At the same time, *Zuikaku* was also putting together what was available for her third strike of the day. This one included five fighters (from two different carriers), two carrier bombers, and seven carrier attack planes (six armed with 800kg bombs and the last to act as a tracker aircraft). The flight was commanded by a lieutenant; the junior status of the flight commander and the small numbers of strike aircraft indicated how savagely the morning strikes had been treated by American defenses.

Between 1320 and 1400hrs, *Zuikaku* and *Junyo* recovered all remaining aircraft, but the Japanese were clearly down to a small number of strike aircraft. *Zuikaku* recovered five Zeros (four from *Junyo*), seven carrier bombers from *Shokaku*, and seven carrier attack planes (six from *Zuikaku* and one from *Shokaku*). *Junyo* landed another nine fighters (one from *Zuikaku*) and six carrier bombers from her first strike. During this time, another two fighters, four carrier bombers and a carrier attack plane were forced to ditch. The recovering aircraft were damaged in many cases and the crews physically exhausted and emotionally drained after their experiences. Nomoto decided that he would not mount a fourth strike. Kakuta pushed his men harder, and ordered another strike before dusk with whatever aircraft could be readied. The best that *Junyo* could do was a strike of six Zeros and four carrier bombers launched at 1535hrs.

Enterprise was able to maintain a CAP over TF-16 which did not really matter since TF-16 had moved beyond Japanese striking range. However, it was impossible to maintain any air cover over TF-17. As TF-16 retreated, *Hornet* and her escorts were left to fend for themselves. After the first attempt to tow *Hornet* was interrupted by a Japanese aircraft feigning a dive-bomb

attack, heavy cruiser *Northampton* returned to rig a new towing line. By 1330hrs, the line was rigged and a speed of three knots achieved. Later, a speed of six knots was reached and Murray headed the crippled carrier to the east.

The Japanese had no intention of letting *Hornet* escape. Throughout the morning, Japanese aircraft monitored the progress of American attempts to salvage the carrier. Since TF-17 had no CAP, *Hornet* remained terribly vulnerable. At 1345hrs, the radar aboard *Northampton* picked up a group of aircraft to the northwest at 103 miles. This was the *Junyo* strike, which continued to linger to the northwest according to the radar track on *Northampton*. Later, at 1400hrs, the cruiser detected another group of aircraft to the northwest at 110 miles. This was the *Zuikaku* strike; both Japanese groups were attempting to find the undamaged American carrier operating to the north of *Hornet* as assessed by Nagumo's staff. Finally, the *Junyo* strike abandoned this fruitless search and headed south. At 1513hrs, the strike leader spotted the damaged *Hornet* and with no other targets in the offing, decided to attack her. With the Japanese aircraft inbound, *Northampton* again cast off her tow line to *Hornet* and prepared to defend the crippled carrier. The six carrier attack planes armed with torpedoes all attacked from the *Hornet*'s starboard side. The strike leader skillfully placed his torpedo just aft of the two previous torpedo hits. The other five torpedoes failed to score, but the one hit was sufficient to increase the list to some 14 degrees and make any successful salvage operation unlikely. The successful torpedo pilot was shot down after his drop, as was another of the Type 97 aircraft. Five Zeros also did not return to *Junyo*. Next to find *Hornet* were the two carrier bombers from *Zuikaku*. These attacked at 1541hrs and scored a near miss.

With the list increasing to 20 degrees, Captain Mason ordered his crew to abandon ship just after the dive-bombing attack. During the early process of abandoning ship, the six *Zuikaku* carrier attack planes operating as level bombers with large 1,760-pound bombs executed an attack run at 1555hrs from 8,000ft off *Hornet*'s port quarter. One of the bombs hit aft on the flight deck but caused little damage. The rest missed astern. The final attack of the day occurred at 1650hrs when *Junyo*'s four carrier bombers arrived on the scene. One of the aircraft scored a hit forward of the island which penetrated the flight deck and exploded on the hangar deck causing a fire.

Hornet's fate was decided. Mason was the last to leave the ship at 1627hrs. After the final air attack, Murray assigned the destroyer *Mustin* the task of sinking *Hornet* while the remaining ships of TF-17 steamed east at

27 knots. *Mustin* fired eight torpedoes into the carrier and four exploded. This did not have the immediate desired effect, so Murray sent destroyer *Anderson* to finish the carrier. She also fired her full load of eight torpedoes, and this time six were seen to explode. Still the carrier would not go down. Now the two destroyers pumped 430 rounds of 5in. shells into the carrier; this caused a fire throughout her length, but the ship still refused to sink. The two American destroyers departed at 2030hrs. At about 2100hrs, Japanese destroyers *Makigumo* and *Akigumo* arrived in the vicinity of *Hornet*. They confirmed her identity and determined the ship was obviously beyond salvage. They fired four more torpedoes into the blazing hulk. *Hornet* finally sank the next day at 0130hrs.

The battle had gone well for the Japanese, but Kondo was determined to capitalize on the success of the day and pursue the Americans throughout the night. At 1804hrs, he ordered his forces to prepare for a night battle and form a scouting line to catch any fleeing or crippled American ships. By this point, Abe's Vanguard Force and Kondo's Advance Force were only a dozen miles apart. Destroyers from the Vanguard Force quickly located the burning *Hornet*. Kondo decided to break off the pursuit at 2300hrs if nothing else was detected. The two remaining Japanese carriers were sent north in preparation for a morning search; results of the search would dictate whether the battle continued or not. The night allowed the Japanese to take stock of their remaining air strength. Losses had been extremely heavy, but 97 aircraft remained aboard the two operational carriers. Aboard *Zuikaku* were 67 aircraft – 38 fighters, ten carrier bombers and 19 carrier attack planes. *Junyo* boasted 12 fighters, 12 carrier bombers and six carrier attack planes.

For the Japanese, the number of American carriers involved in the battle remained unclear. The early consensus was three, though no Japanese aviator had seen three separate American carriers. Nomoto discerned this after personally debriefing the crews of returning scout planes. Kakuta thought there were three, and reported at about 1830hrs that all were sunk or badly damaged. Yamamoto weighed in at 1950hrs with an assessment that four carriers had been attacked and that one had sunk and the other three were badly damaged. This was also Nagumo's view. All were sure that the "Naval Battle of the South Pacific" was a great victory.

The air searches on the morning of October 27 revealed nothing, so after conducting a search for downed aviators in the area of the attacks on *Hornet* and *Enterprise*, Kondo headed his forces north. The wounded *Shokaku* and *Zuiho* returned to Truk on October 28, and the rest of the Japanese fleet arrived on October 30. The American forces were already in port when the Japanese dropped anchor at Truk. By the morning of October 27, TF-16 was northeast of Espiritu Santo with TF-17 close astern. On the afternoon of the next day, TF-61 arrived in the waters of Noumea.

The Japanese claimed a great victory with three carriers, one battleship, one cruiser, one destroyer, and one unidentified large warship sunk and 79 American aircraft destroyed (plus those that went down with the sunken carriers). This was obviously excessive, but the real losses were severe enough. *Hornet* was sunk along with the destroyer *Porter*. *Enterprise* was damaged, as was the battleship *South Dakota*, light cruiser *San Juan*, and destroyers *Smith* and *Mahan* (damaged in a collision with *South Dakota* while exiting the battle area on October 27). Of the 175 aircraft at the start of the battle on the two carriers, 80 were lost to all causes (33 fighters, 28 dive-bombers and 19 Avengers).

Japanese losses were also heavy. Three ships were badly damaged and would require extensive repairs in Japan – carriers *Shokaku* and *Zuiho* and heavy cruiser *Chikuma*. The real loss to the Japanese was in aircraft, and even more importantly, in aircrew. Of the 203 aircraft that they began the battle with, almost half (99) were destroyed. Losses were particularly heavy in strike aircraft with 41 of 63 carrier bombers and 30 of 57 carrier attack planes destroyed. The primary agent of destruction was for the first time in a carrier battle evenly split between American CAP (26) and antiaircraft fire (25). The balance of Japanese bomber losses was from ditching and operational losses (18) and one destroyed when *Shokaku* was bombed.

Aircraft were relatively easy to replace, but trained aircrews were another matter. The Japanese lost 145 aircrew – 68 pilots and 77 observers during the battle. To show the severity of these losses, it should be kept in mind that total aircrew loss at Midway was only 110. An additional aspect of the Santa Cruz losses was that among the 145 aircrew lost were 23 section, squadron, or air group leaders (in the IJN, leaders could be either pilots or observers). This had obvious short-term and long-term implications for the state of Japanese carrier aviation. In return, the Americans lost only a total of 22 aircrew.

ANALYSIS OF THE BATTLE

Santa Cruz featured the finest Japanese carrier air attack on an American carrier task force of the war. Overall, the Japanese clearly demonstrated that they remained the masters of massing carrier air power. A total of 138 aircraft were committed (42 Zeros, 57 carrier bombers, 36 carrier attack planes and three contact planes) in the initial assault on TF-61. All of these attacked an American carrier formation, though not all attacked the carrier itself. The combination of the Type 97 carrier attack plane with the Type 91 air-launched torpedo was proven again to be a formidable ship-killer. Zeros performed well in the escort role.

The Japanese had taken the lessons from Midway and applied them well. Attention to damage control and improved damage control procedures were far superior as shown by the survival of *Shokaku*. CAP performance was also much better since aircraft were positioned at various altitudes and were actually given advance notice of incoming American strike aircraft. However, it's important to note that the Japanese CAP was unable to stop or even seriously disrupt the one strike group which found the Japanese carriers. A critical mistake at Midway was the sloppy planning given to searches. At Santa Cruz, much greater attention was paid to scouting and even the Americans admitted that the performance of Japanese scout aircraft was superior. The Japanese tactic of using the Vanguard Force as an advanced screen to the carriers proved successful, and was commented favorably upon by several after-action American reports.

The Americans still showed an inability to coordinate air strikes and successfully mass carrier air power. This was the result of flawed doctrine and persistent communications problems. Added to this was the poor level of training shown by CAG-10. The result was a series of piecemeal attacks, most against secondary targets. Most damning was the fact that of the two strikes launched, only ten aircraft out of 75 managed to attack their primary target, the flight deck of a Japanese carrier. American torpedo aircraft remained ineffective.

American fighter defense was the most controversial aspect of the battle. The performance of TF-61's FDO was viewed as ineffective from Halsey on down. The reasons for this were many. A major factor was inadequate warning owing primarily to radar problems on the carriers. Accordingly, the Wildcats were positioned at 10,000ft to save fuel and oxygen. This was seen as a mistake after the battle, especially given the Wildcat's inability to climb quickly. After-action reports also commented that the air battles were taking place too close to the carriers. Instead of the desired 20 miles away, air engagements at Santa Cruz were occurring only a few miles from the carriers which meant there was insufficient distance to complete the destruction of approaching Japanese formations. Overarching all these problems was a continuing issue with communications. All these lessons were digested and put to good effect later in war. Eventually, American fast carrier task forces gained a high measure of protection from conventional massed Japanese air attack. Santa Cruz was the last time in the war that skillful Japanese carrier aviators could press home their attacks in a determined manner and cause serious damage to an American carrier task force.

AFTERMATH

Despite the undeniable Japanese victory, it was an incomplete triumph. The escape of *Enterprise* prevented the battle from being a total American disaster and stopped the Japanese from turning a tactical success into a strategic one. *Enterprise*'s survival was key as she was repaired enough to return to the campaign in November when she played a key role in repelling the next (and final) Japanese onslaught. The terrible attrition exacted by the Americans against Japanese carrier aviators meant that the Japanese were not able to follow up their advantage by using their decimated air groups to attack American airpower on Henderson Field.

Another result of the battle was effectively to remove the Japanese carrier fleet from the Guadalcanal campaign. *Shokaku* and *Zuiho* were forced back to Japan for repairs, and the Japanese elected to send back *Zuikaku* as well to rebuild her air group. This was a further demonstration of the inflexibility of the Japanese carrier air group system which prevented the shuffling of aircraft from one ship to another. Taking into account surviving aircraft from both *Shokaku* and *Zuikaku*, added to the largely unaffected air group

Henderson Field on Guadalcanal pictured in 1942. Possession of this airfield gave the Americans control of the waters around Guadalcanal during the day and eventually decided the entire campaign in their favor. (Naval History and Heritage Command)

from *Hiyo*, sufficient aircraft clearly existed to give *Zuikaku* a full air group, had the Japanese decided that her continued presence in the area was critical. Since *Hiyo* was still immobilized at Truk, this left only *Junyo* for the next phase of the campaign. It is hard to understand why Yamamoto continued like this, unless he truly believed that the claims of three American carriers sunk at Santa Cruz were authentic and that he would not face any carriers in the next phase.

Santa Cruz was the forgotten carrier battle of 1942. Despite the myth, the Japanese carrier force was not destroyed at Midway – proven by the fact that the Japanese were able to gain a tactical victory at Santa Cruz and came very close to scoring a strategic one. The results of the battle were generally favorable for the Japanese, but they paid a very high price in aircraft and aircrew which prevented them from following up their victory. Santa Cruz was the best performance of the Japanese carrier force during the war. However, it came at such a cost that the next time the Japanese carrier would enter battle was June 1944. The price paid by the Americans was high, but ultimately necessary. The next and decisive phase of the Guadalcanal campaign in November was fought without the threat of a large Japanese carrier force. Possession of Henderson Field was ultimately the key to victory and the Japanese inability to neutralize or seize the airfield eventually forced them to admit defeat and evacuate Guadalcanal in February 1943.

BIBLIOGRAPHY

There are surprisingly few books focused on the Guadalcanal carrier battles. These additional resources are recommended for further insights into the battles.

Dull, Paul S., *A Battle History of the Imperial Japanese Navy 1941–45*, Naval Institute Press: Annapolis, Maryland, 1978

Frank, Richard B., *Guadalcanal*, Random House: New York, 1990

Hammel, Eric, *Guadalcanal: The Carrier Battles*, Crown Publishers: New York, 1987

_____, *Carrier Strike*, Pacifica Press: Pacifica, California, 1999

Lundstrom, John B., *The First Team and the Guadalcanal Campaign*, Naval Institute Press: Annapolis, Maryland, 1994

_____, *Black Shoe Carrier Admiral*, Naval Institute Press: Annapolis, Maryland, 2006

Morison, Samuel Eliot, *The Struggle for Guadalcanal* (*Volume V of The History of United States Naval Operations in World War II*), Little, Brown and Company: Boston, 1975

www.combinedfleet.com

The following Osprey titles are also useful for additional background to the battles:

Stille, Mark, New Vanguard 109: *Imperial Japanese Navy Aircraft Carriers 1921–45*, Osprey Publishing Ltd: Oxford, 2005

_____, New Vanguard 114: *US Navy Aircraft Carriers 1922–45 (Prewar classes)*, Osprey Publishing Ltd: Oxford, 2005

_____, Duel 6: *USN Carriers vs. IJN Carriers*, Osprey Publishing Ltd: Oxford, 2007

_____, Campaign 214: *The Coral Sea 1942*, Osprey Publishing Ltd: Oxford, 2009

_____, Campaign 226: *Midway 1942*, Osprey Publishing Ltd: Oxford, 2010

INDEX